CARING FOR YOUR SOUL
IN MATTERS OF MONEY®

CARING
FOR YOUR
SOUL
in
MATTERS OF MONEY®

KAREN RAMSEY, CFP®
WITH WARD SERRILL

*Give your gift —
to the world —*

Karen Ramsey

TIRE
SWING
BOOKS

FIRST EDITION
Book design by Paulette Eickman

Library of Congress Control Number: 2006909655
Library of Congress Cataloging-in-Publication Data
on file at the Library of Congress

To Lydia and Annie—the greatest gifts of my life.

But I want first of all—in fact, as an end to these other desires—to be at peace with myself. I want a singleness of eye, a purity of intention, a central core to my life that will enable me to carry out these obligations and activities as well as I can. I want, in fact—to borrow from the language of the saints—to live "in grace" as much of the time as possible. I am not using this term in a strictly theological sense. By grace I mean an inner harmony, essentially spiritual, which can be translated into outward harmony. I am seeking perhaps what Socrates asked for in the prayer from the Phaedrus when he said, "May the outward and inward man be at one." I would like to achieve a state of inner spiritual grace from which I could function and give as I was meant to in the eye of God.

ANNE MORROW LINDBERGH, *Gift from the Sea*

TABLE OF CONTENTS

INTRODUCTION

*F*or most of my life I worked hard, excessively hard. It was the only way I knew how to live. And yet, despite long hours and dedication, I could never really get ahead financially. It seemed as though some invisible force held me in its grasp. My response to this was to work even harder and resign myself to the fact that struggling about money was just a fact of life.

Then I came across a book that changed my entire outlook. Professor Jacob Needleman, in *Money and the Meaning of Life*, talked about money from a philosophical point of view. He inquired into the role of money in the search for our ultimate purpose, our meaning in life.

I had never considered that money could have a deeper purpose. Money symbolized a never-ending source of struggle to me. How could it help me uncover a deeper meaning to my life? The soul searching that followed over the next few years led me to question everything I had ever been taught about work and money. It eventually led me to discover my true life's work and, ultimately, to this book.

In exploring my deeper attitudes and beliefs around money, I came to discover core subconscious beliefs about money that I learned in childhood and that had run my life without my even knowing. I call these beliefs my *money baggage*. It was this money baggage that was responsible for my incessant struggles around money, my working hard but never feeling like I had more than just enough to squeak by.

Once I began my practice as a CERTIFIED FINANCIAL PLANNER™ professional, I saw that I was not alone in struggling over money. Nearly everyone I spent time with shared these troubles, and it made no difference how much money they had. From millionaires to waitresses, they were all wrestling with core issues around money. With some people, their struggles were obvious: they were worried where the next check was going to come from or how they would pay for their children to go to college. With others it was more subtle, a nagging kind of worry that there wouldn't be enough. Many people did not want to deal with money at all; they preferred avoidance. Others never were able to make ends meet no matter how hard they worked. And still others had plenty of money but weren't happy or couldn't stop working themselves to the bone. Young or old, rich or poor, every person I knew was struggling with money.

As I met with each of them I came to realize that each had their own unique money baggage they were carrying around. Each was operating on a belief system about money, handed to them as children. And, like me, they had unknowingly built their lives in complete alignment with these deeper beliefs.

As I helped individuals examine these deeper beliefs, they became consciously aware for the first time that their struggles over money were not innate, that they were not carved in stone. Rather, their experiences with money were born from a deeply held thought. As they learned to change their thoughts around money, their lives began to change, first inwardly and then outwardly.

Once these burdens of outworn beliefs and attitudes about money were brought into the light, I found that people had something else within them, a deeply resonant passion in their lives, some driving force pulling them toward what they wanted to do. I saw it so often that I now consider it universal. There is within everyone at a deep level a desire to live a more purposeful and meaningful life.

What holds most people back is not that they are unable to identify their passions and dreams and deeply held interests. It's that, once defined, those dreams don't seem attainable. There is always some obstacle—a feeling of unworth; a fear of leaving the familiar; conflicting feelings about being successful; a fear that those dreams wouldn't be lucrative enough. So back they go inside the limitation of their money baggage where they continue to struggle over money.

For more than a dozen years now, I have led workshops to help people examine their relationship to money, deconstruct their limiting belief systems, and understand how to bring money in line with their deepest passions.

Each of us has a custom-made gift to give to the world. A gift based on our distinctive background, abilities, values, passions, commitments, and concerns. A gift that is a joy to give, an expression of who we truly are. A gift that inspires others and brings a purpose to our life. A gift the world needs. I believe our soul knows what our gift is. When we listen, we discover that gift. When we find the courage to give that gift to the world, we are caring for our soul.

Jacob Needleman says, *"It means finding the precise place of money at the heart of the most important undertaking of our lives—the search to become what we are meant to be, in the service of that greatness that calls to every man or woman on this endangered earth."*

Why does your soul matter in money? It matters because money affects everything in your life. And your life is sacred. Your soul wants you to do more than just survive; it wants you to live an authentic and purposeful life. Your soul is that voice deep inside you asking you to find meaningful work, and to do that work empowered by love and awareness, fully confident that the resources you want and need are available to you.

Only by incorporating the soul into our lives and, therefore, into our relationship with money, will we set fear to the side and gain a measure of that peace of mind, joy, and happiness we so often hear about but rarely experience.

This book is about taking a journey to where money and soul intersect. It is about diving below the surface to discover our inner-most beliefs about money and transform those beliefs so money can do what money was meant to do: help us make the world a better and more loving place.

In Part I of this book, you will explore and discover your own money baggage and understand how it affects most areas of your life. In Part II, you will learn how to create a new money message and begin a new future around this more empowered vision of your life.

This process is about making our subconscious beliefs and the attitudes we have about money more conscious. Then using this newfound consciousness, we can craft a more powerful and confident life that is fully consistent with the deep potential of our soul.

PART I
MONEY BAGGAGE

—

CHAPTER 1

OUR PERSONAL MONEY BAGGAGE

*E*ach of us carries around money baggage. This baggage is crammed full of the experiences, ideas, and beliefs about money that we had as children. It is stuffed to the brim with the attitudes about money our parents and other adults in our lives had and what they taught us through their actions or words.

Everyone has money baggage. Everyone. I don't care how rich or poor, what race or nationality, whether spiritual or not. Everyone in your family has money baggage. All your friends carry some. Everyone you work with does too. As we'll discuss later, even Dorothy in *The Wizard of Oz* had money baggage.

Our money baggage is a decision about money that we formed in childhood. It is based on something we experienced, were told, heard, or observed. Early on, something happened to us. We were taught something about money, or we heard adults talking about it, or found out it was something you *don't* talk about, or we saw something that led us to make a conclusion about it that we treated as fact. And we did it without awareness, without realizing we were doing it. We considered it true and we made our lives conform to it without question.

You might, for example, believe that you have to work hard to make money. That you aren't supposed to talk about money. That it is wrong to have too much. That you can never have enough because you can lose it at any time. You might believe deep down that you don't deserve money, or that money is bad or that you're not supposed to spend it on yourself.

These ideas about money are ingrained in us. We accept them as truth, the way the world is. And to the extent these beliefs go unexamined, they are responsible for affecting every decision we have ever made about money. They affect the job we have, the savings we do or don't have, the way we spend money, what we spend it on, and whom we spend it with.

If you unconsciously believe deep down that you don't really deserve money, that you aren't good enough to enjoy abundance, guess what? That may be the reason you don't get the raise you want, or never win that lucrative contract, or are always struggling to make ends meet. Or perhaps you acquire plenty of money but something always comes up and it is gone before you know what happened, either by spending it or giving it away. Deep down you are telling yourself that you don't deserve it, and the universe is simply listening to that deeper voice and giving you precisely what you believe.

If you were taught that women aren't good with money, that may be the reason you married a man who would provide for you and handle all the financial details in your life. If you believe that money is bad, maybe it makes sense that you don't have enough, or can't hold onto it, or attract situations that require more money than you expected to spend. If you saw a relative using money to control the family, maybe you vowed to become financially independent, never relying on anyone else—and perhaps you carry that independence over to parts of your life you never intended, and find yourself unable to maintain a long-term intimate relationship.

Our money baggage takes root deep in our subconscious. It is so deeply underground that we do not question it; we don't even know it is there. In my workshops, some people will cross their arms and tell me emphatically that they don't have money baggage or that they can't identify it. But for those who keep working and do the exercises, their money baggage eventually appears. It is always there.

From listening to hundreds of people's stories, I have identified the seven most common money baggage themes (some people may have more than one of these):

I don't deserve money.

There will never be enough.

Money is bad.

I have to work hard to make money.

I can't depend on anyone else.

Money equals security.

Money determines my self-worth.

Because money affects everything in our lives, our money baggage affects our finances, our relationships, the house we live in, the job we have, and even our health. In later chapters we'll see specifically how and why.

As you read the stories in this book, begin to reflect upon your own earliest memories about money. In those memories you will find a blueprint of your current life and the specific struggles you have around money. What shaped your childhood? What conclusions and decisions did you make about money that are still silently driving your life today?

As you reflect on these matters, your money baggage may become obvious to you, and if it does, use WORKSHEET 3: DISCOVERING MY MONEY BAGGAGE to write it down. But if you are like most people, it won't be so readily apparent; you will need to dig a little for it. The chapters ahead will help with that. Whenever it comes to you, write it down; give it words; claim it as your own. This important act of claiming your money baggage is the first step toward living a life consistent with your highest beliefs about money and finding your soul's true calling.

CHAPTER 2

⌒

DISCOVERING MY OWN MONEY BAGGAGE

*M*ost of my adult life you could have described me as a workaholic. Sixty-hour workweeks were standard. I was always the first to arrive and the last to go home at night, regardless of the job. I could never do enough. And yet, despite working long hours at good paying jobs, I never had more than just enough to get by.

I grew up on a farm in Loveland, Colorado, where we didn't have inside plumbing until I was in third grade. My dad got up at four-thirty in the morning to milk the cows, seven days a week. He would work in the wheat, barley, or alfalfa fields all day and be back in the barn at five o'clock at night to milk the cows a second time. He'd come in for dinner. He'd eat. He'd sit in his easy chair exhausted and fall asleep. Around nine he'd get up and go to bed. At four-thirty the next morning he was up milking the cows again.

I remember wishing my dad would play with me, but he never had time for playing. If he wasn't milking the cows, he was driving the tractor in the fields or working on the machinery. It seemed like the only time I spent with him was going to town to get a part for some machinery that was broken. I secretly hoped something would break so we could go to town together, a guilty wish since I knew fixing it would cost money, which was in short supply.

I remember only one vacation in my entire childhood, three days at a cabin in the mountains. I dreaded hearing my friends describe their vacations, praying they wouldn't ask me what I did. Playing on our tire swing and reading library books always paled in comparison to their vacation activities. I wanted to fit in but knew I never would.

While my dad was tending the farm, I saw my mother work equally hard, raising us, taking care of everyone, and making sure that we had three square meals on the table each day.

Growing up in this environment, I made a conclusion about life that, years later, I came to recognize as the first part of my money baggage. What I learned through observing everything around me was *you have to work really hard.*

But working hard is not the only thing I learned from my parents. I also observed how the constant struggle with money issues affected our lives, and this became the second part of my money baggage. Let me explain.

August meant harvest time on the farm. My father had the wheat and barley trucked to the granary. On settlement day, we received a check for the tonnage of grain delivered.

It was the happiest day of the year, and it started with a trip to the bank. The whole family drove five miles from the granary in Loveland to the town of Berthoud to deposit the check. We'd go out for an ice-cream cone afterward—something we didn't usually do. I vividly remember riding in the back of my parents' blue 1954 Ford, with the wind in my hair and feeling that everything was right in the world.

Months later, in January, February, or March, I would see my father at his desk poring over papers, sorting bills, running his hands through his hair, trying to make ends meet. His shoulders would be slumped and he'd shake his head a lot. Eventually he would throw his pencil down, push his chair back from the desk, and say, "Well, we just have to go to the bank and get a loan to make it through until harvest." I could see the anguish in his eyes and, although he never said it aloud, I knew he felt like a failure.

In the kitchen, I saw my mother crying. I loved my mom so much. I wanted her to be happy and it broke my heart to see her cry.

It made me feel alone and really sad for her. And scared—scared that we wouldn't have enough to eat, that my parents wouldn't ever be happy again, that I'd never have a life like other kids, that life wasn't going to turn out.

The ride on this second trip to the bank, to borrow the money to get us through until the next harvest, felt much different. The three of us rode in silence: my father gripping the steering wheel and clenching his jaw; my mom looking out the window with a resigned look on her face; and me in the back seat, hoping she wouldn't start crying again.

Every year, this boom and bust cycle repeated itself. Happiness on settlement day; fear, sadness, and frustration on loan day.

I vividly remember the day my dad sold the farm. To get out from under the debt that had accumulated over the years, he was forced to hand it over to a banker from Denver who wore fancy cowboy boots that had probably never seen the inside of a barn. From a distance, I saw him hand my dad the check for the farm and, even from where I stood, I could see the relief in my dad's face— finally he could get out of debt. But I knew deep inside he was humiliated to have "lost" the family farm. From that moment on we were tenant farmers—living on the farm that had been in my dad's family for more than forty years. But instead of my dad working hard to make money for us, he was doing it for the rich businessman.

From watching and experiencing all of this, the second part of my money baggage emerged. I concluded *there is never enough.* I put these two innocent conclusions about money together at an early age and they became my money baggage: *You have to work hard to make money, and even if you do, you'll never make enough.* This simple and erroneous conclusion became the unconscious burden I carried around for the next thirty-plus years of my life.

I lived the only way I knew how to live: by working hard. I excelled academically. I joined the band and honor society. I was editor of the yearbook. On top of all this, from ninth grade on I worked twelve to sixteen hours a week in the lab of our local hospital cleaning test tubes. I tried to pretend that my family had money but—even if I fooled my classmates—I knew deep down it wasn't true.

I carried my money baggage into adulthood. I worked hard and put myself through college, got good grades, and found my first job soon after graduating. I was the ideal employee, working my tail off, coming in early, and staying late. I worked through lunch. My boss knew if there was a job to do, I'd get it done no matter what it took. For me, that's just what you did in life—work hard. It's how life was. Working hard wasn't a conscious choice for me. It was a given—no questions asked.

I didn't notice I was still "driving the tractor" from sunup to sundown. It was so automatic for me to work hard that the thought of not working hard made me panic. I thought I could lose everything at any time if I didn't stay at it.

Despite my hard work and the fact that I made pretty good money, I was always haunted by the feeling I'd have to make that drive to the bank for a loan. Deep down I knew there wouldn't be enough money to get me through. So I worked even harder. I started a business consulting practice and worked sixty to seventy hours a week. I went in early, I paid all the bills, and I arranged all the appointments. I prepped for client pitch meetings or for the consulting work.

While I was doing all this work, it seemed that my business partner, Nita, was always in one of three places: getting her nails or hair done, playing with her kids, or working out. I'd pick her up, we'd do the two or three hours of consulting with the client, and I'd drop her off at home. Then I'd go back to work. This went on for a year and a half.

Finally the day came when I said, "Nita, this isn't working for me."

Nita, looking a bit confused, said, "What isn't working for you?"

"Our business partnership—it isn't fair. I'm working all these hours, but we both get paid the same. I work before and after you, getting ready for our client work, doing all this extra stuff...and then you just *waltz* in to do the consulting work. I'm working way more than you are," I snapped.

Nita wasn't the least impressed. She said, "Karen, it's because you have it completely wired up that you have to work hard. I don't. And even if I did work harder, you'd find a way to work just as hard as you are now. You'd find something else that had to be done. I let you do all that work, because you feel like you have to do it."

"And it's even worse than that, Karen," she said. "Some people make a lot more than we do and they work a lot fewer hours. Maybe it's not all about working hard."

"Of course it is, Nita. How else can we have a successful business and make enough to support ourselves?" I replied indignantly.

I didn't want to hear any more. I drove her the rest of the way home in silence. After dropping Nita off, I started to argue with her in the empty car. "How dare you say that to me? How the heck can you make money and not work hard?"

But Nita's words haunted me. I respected her and her opinion enough that, even though I didn't like what she'd said, I knew there had to be some truth in it. I'd seen my mom and dad work themselves to exhaustion and, trusting in them as role models, I didn't know any other way. If working hard was not the answer, then what was?

Soon after this conversation, Nita and I closed our consulting practice and I took a job as a human resources director at an ad agency. Guess what? I worked really hard and very long hours . . . and never had more than enough money.

I remember being at a stoplight after another twelve-hour day thinking my usual: *If I keep working I'll be able to retire someday. I just have to make it through the next twenty-six years.* I noticed how tightly my hands were gripping the steering wheel and how tense my shoulders were. The appalling reality of this future was weighing down on me.

I began to think about how my early life and experiences around money had shaped my adult life. I suddenly realized that although it was me behind the wheel, my money baggage was the real driver in my life. The idea—that I had to work hard and, no matter what, there would not be enough—was in control, not me.

Over the next few months, I began to get glimpses of how powerful and pervasive the conclusions I had made as a child were, and how strongly they influenced me. *You have to work hard to make money, and even if you do, you'll never make enough* had led to an endless cycle of work and worry and fear. As I was looking out the window one day, pondering this, a question kept running through my mind, "What should I do with my life?"

I knew I had always been interested in the role money played in my life choices, so I decided to take some courses in financial planning. I found it so interesting that I continued to study and take more classes. I worked hard at it (naturally) and became a CERTIFIED FINANCIAL PLANNER™ professional. I hired a career counselor to help me develop a business plan and a marketing strategy. Three months later, I opened up a financial planning practice.

I was thrilled to be doing financial planning, something I loved to do. But I still found that life stubbornly held on to its tendency to make my money baggage come true.

My income would rise and fall on a monthly basis in direct correlation with my expenses. When I had a good revenue month, my expenses would also be high—the copier would break or quarterly taxes would come due. So I would eagerly look forward to the months when it looked like my overhead would be low, thinking if my revenue stayed high, I'd start to get ahead. But it never happened that way. In low-expense months, my revenue would dip, almost as if by magic, leaving me with my usual sense of scarcity. No matter what I did or how I planned, I could not get ahead. I could not shake my underlying fear that, even if I worked like crazy, *there wouldn't be enough.*

My circumstances had developed in perfect harmony with my money baggage. It was as if my money baggage was the background music that had played in every scene of my life.

Discovering your own money baggage is the first step toward overcoming your struggles around money. It is not hard work to do. It's just that most of us have never had our attention drawn to it. We have never explored our beliefs about money because we consider our beliefs to be complete fact, "just the way life is." But you will find, as you do this work, that your money baggage is not true. You have simply lived your life in alignment with an erroneous decision you made as a child. Given that you've never examined your life in this way before, it's easy to see how that could have occurred.

In the chapters that follow, you will learn the three basic principles that underlie your money baggage. You'll also examine questions that will reveal to you your own money baggage and how it has shaped every part of your life. Later on, you will learn about creating a new money message. By living your life in a way that is consistent with this new message, you will begin to manifest your dreams.

~

CHAPTER 3

MONEY BAGGAGE PRINCIPLE #1:
OUR MONEY BAGGAGE IS FORMED IN CHILDHOOD

*M*oney baggage is the decision about money that we made when we were children. Early on, something happened to us or we were taught something about money or we saw something that led us to make a conclusion about it. We took this conclusion to be fact. Throughout our lives we have taken actions consistent with this decision about money and these actions have shaped our lives. These actions, though arising from a false belief, influence our current attitudes and relationships with money.

From our early experiences, our money baggage might be:

Money is scarce; we can't afford it.

I don't deserve it.

Rich people are mean.

Money is not something to be talked about.

Girls are not good with money.

I shouldn't spend money on myself.

It's not okay to want things.

Save for a rainy day.

Get a good paying job.

If I am an artist, I'll be poor.

Be responsible.

Money is power.

The message may not have been verbal, but we got the message just the same. From our observations and experiences, we formed conclusions about money that have run our lives ever since.

Everyone you know has money baggage. As I mentioned in the Introduction, even Dorothy in *The Wizard of Oz* has some. Let's take a look at what conclusions Dorothy might have made about work and money.

As you know, Dorothy lived on a farm in Kansas with her dog Toto, and she found people around her too busy to deal with her.

The story opens with Dorothy running onto the farm excitedly to tell Auntie Em about mean old Miss Gulch hitting Toto for running in her garden after her cat. But Auntie Em and Uncle Henry are too busy to listen and can't be interrupted: the incubator has conked out and they have to count the chicks and get them into another pen. Dorothy urgently tries to convey the importance of what's happened, saying that Miss Gulch has threatened to get the sheriff, but Auntie Em, preoccupied with her work, finally just tells Dorothy to be helpful and stay out of trouble.

This scene alone is enough to conclude that Dorothy might be getting the message that chickens (work and money) are more important than she is. This idea is reinforced later when she falls into the hog pen and hits her head. She is pulled out and is being tended to by the farmhands when Auntie Em comes over and threatens to fire them for "all this jabberwocky." When they try to tell her about Dorothy getting hurt, Aunt Em will have nothing to do with it. She hustles them back to work because work is more important.

If we assume Dorothy grew up around this attitude and behavior over the years, it's also safe to assume she might have ended up with some definite ideas about how much higher work ranks in the family than she does.

Few of us grew up on farms, but we might recognize the issue. How many of us learned early on that work and money took time away from the family? That work always came first. Being children, we took everything personally. If we did not get the attention, time, or love we wanted, it must have been because there was something else more important than us. Or we may have decided that there was something wrong with us. Or that we did not deserve love or attention. Whatever conclusion we made, we made it deeply; it formed the basis of our life.

Dorothy's story goes on to illustrate another money baggage lesson that might have also informed her view of the world. When mean Miss Gulch storms into the farmhouse, she carries in her hand an order from the sheriff to take Toto away. Dorothy sees her aunt and uncle buckle under, and to her horror, they hand Toto over to Miss Gulch. But not before Auntie Em gives Miss Gulch a talking to, outlining her despicable qualities and noting that she only got that order from the sheriff because she owns half the county.

So what might Dorothy learn about the world seeing this? Miss Gulch may be the only rich person Dorothy ever knew. From her child's point of view it would appear that money meant power and that rich people were mean. If you had money, you could even get the sheriff to take your dog away. How might something like this affect Dorothy later in life?

As we will see as we discover how money baggage works, someone who believes that money makes a person mean might end up creating a life where he or she becomes an honest, hardworking person but never allows himself or herself to have much money, for fear of becoming a bad person.

What exactly is money baggage? It is the set of beliefs you gained in childhood about money, which now operate subconsciously as automatic behaviors and attitudes in your life. And these behaviors and attitudes dictate all of your decisions about money. We create innocent but mistaken ideas about money and these ideas end up coloring our existence for as long as we let them.

I met Oliver in one of my workshops. He is a wonderful, warm, and caring man. He is one of the happiest people I know. Oliver had to do a lot of work uncovering some painful childhood memories before he could discover his money baggage.

He was one of nine children from a poor family living in Austria. They lived mostly off of their garden and wild mushrooms and berries they gathered from the forest. His father, a Jew in war-torn Austria, got what work he could, often working at night for a friend at great risk to both of them, for, as Oliver explained, it was illegal during World War II to hire Jews.

⸻

My first memories about money are of my parents going over their monthly grocery bill. We had a monthly charge account at the grocery store in town. There were two little hardcover books in which every item would be written down. One book stayed at the store and the other we took home with us.

At the end of the month my mother would pick up the book at the store to compare it to the one at home, and my parents would go down the list. It always started very civilized. After a few items my dad would find something that he would question. He would always find something!

My mother would explain things, my father's voice would get louder, his face would turn red, and he would start to yell. My mother would begin to cry, and then my grandmother would give a big sigh and carry me from the room.

Outside the closed door I listened to my father yelling and mistreating my mother despite her pleading to stop. I wanted to protect her, but I didn't know how. I was three years old, scared, alone, and helpless.

This scene, to varying degrees of intensity, happened regularly all through my childhood.

I saw that people got angry and upset and fought about money. It was scary, because there was always something wrong. I decided *this is no place for me. I'm leaving.*

Oliver's money baggage became: *We don't have the money, something is always wrong! I'm out of here!* This was not a conscious thought, as an adult might have. It became part of his subconscious imprinting, his inherent idea about how the world works. For sixty years Oliver did everything he could to avoid dealing with money, because as a child, he decided money meant pain.

We have all followed the same process that Oliver did. We took a thought about money and we built our life around it. The messages we got might have been different but the process was the same.

Oliver began to uncover his money baggage at age sixty, but it was not easy. He had to remember a lot of difficult memories. And he had to look at how his attitudes about money had kept him in painful situations for most of his life.

Money baggage has such a hold on us because the power of association is at work inside our brains. We associate money with the emotions we had around childhood experiences and the wounds caused by difficult times or traumatic events. Over time we forget the experiences but not the associations; as adults we continue to react to them.

Maybe we saw someone mistreat another person over money or dominate them and we concluded that *money is bad*. Well, money itself was not what was bad; it was that person's actions. But as kids we were unable to make that distinction. We were discovering the world for the first time. And in that world we decided that money caused pain. It was a bad thing.

What shaped your childhood? What conclusions and decisions did you make about money that are still silently driving your life today? What have you heard about money? What are your earliest memories of money? What did your parents say about money—whether out loud or not? Did they fight about it? What do you say about money today? The answers to these questions are going to give you clues about your own personal money baggage.

Start the process of discovering your money baggage using WORKSHEET 1: MONEY IN MY YOUNGER YEARS in the Appendix. Write down your earliest memories about money. Ask your sister or brother about what it was like growing up and what they learned about money. If your parents are still alive, ask them to talk about their deeper beliefs about money. Try to remember the first time you wanted money or you earned it or spent it. Take a trip back to your childhood home if you can, or look at old photos—anything that might give you a clue or stimulate your memory about the conclusions you made about money. Even if it doesn't come at first, keep at it. You'll find it—everyone has money baggage—and you'll find it by exploring your childhood.

～

CHAPTER 4

MONEY BAGGAGE PRINCIPLE #2:
OUR MONEY BAGGAGE AFFECTS EVERY ASPECT OF OUR LIVES

*O*ur money baggage directs our lives. It determines the clothes we wear, the house we live in, the career we have, the size of our paycheck and savings account. Our money baggage can even determine the friends we have and the partner we choose. It takes us shopping, chooses the car we drive and, in the case of a woman in one of my workshops, even determined the temperature she kept her apartment.

Sally had two visible scars above the collar of her sweater, one on her neck and another on her chin. As I started to talk about money baggage and its origins in childhood, she became noticeably uncomfortable and introverted. While others in the class laughed at some of the things being said, she grew more serious. She was putting a lot of energy into keeping her emotions in check.

When the time came in the workshop to share her money baggage with the group, Sally said: *I can't have any more money, I've already used more than my allotment.*

When Sally was a very young child, she was involved in a car accident and was burned over much of her body. It was severe enough that she had to be in the hospital a very long time. Her parents loved her dearly, and committed their lives to help her and care for her through this trauma. But constant and expensive medical intervention eventually wiped her parents out financially.

Sally saw all of this happening. She saw the effect her accident had on the family. They had to move out of their home and rent an apartment. They had to sell many of their possessions. They no longer took vacations. Toys at Christmas became fewer and smaller. Her parents never talked about it. They never complained or made her feel at all like she was the cause of it. But her young mind saw differently and Sally made a powerful conclusion.

She decided that she had already used up her allotment in life. Her accident had taken too much; it had used up too much money and had caused the family to become deprived.

As an adult Sally never turned the heat up in her apartment above sixty degrees. Instead, she wore a lot of sweaters like the heavy one she wore in class. She rarely if ever went out for meals. She never treated herself to anything.

This woman was shivering in her apartment because of an accident she had as a little girl. She didn't turn up the heat in her apartment because she felt so much guilt at what her parents went through due to her injury. She associated money with pain. She couldn't spend it on herself because she felt she did not deserve any more.

It's not like her parents told her, "Hey, you used up your allotment." They never did anything but try to give her the help and love she deserved. The last thing they wanted was to make her feel guilty. But she saw the financial burden she had become. She saw what her accident did to the family, what they could no longer do afterwards. Her mom had to work harder and take a second job. Sally knew it was because of her.

Through adulthood, friends visiting Sally's apartment would think she had a little idiosyncrasy about keeping her apartment heat down and wearing sweaters all the time. It had nothing to do with that. And it wasn't that she couldn't afford it. Rather, she couldn't spend five or ten dollars more a month on heat because her money baggage would not let her spend money on herself.

Money baggage can even keep us from finding work. A man named David walked into one of my workshops several years back—I'll never forget him. He looked completely downtrodden and wore frumpy, tattered, tweedy looking clothes. Middle-aged, skeletal of frame, plain and simple, he slumped in his chair. He gave the impression he was trying to make himself physically smaller so he wouldn't take up much space. He looked down at the floor most of the time, held his hands, and tapped his feet a lot. He looked like he didn't have a dime.

David was an accounts payable clerk at a shipping company. He'd worked there nine years but didn't like his job very much. He had taken classes to explore other employment options, but he couldn't figure out what else to do. He decided it was his lot in life to just keep working where he was.

He shared with the group that his parents were really poor and he was an only child. He grew up alone; he didn't have a lot of friends.

When it was time to share his money baggage he said, in a voice nearly inaudible: *If you couldn't afford me, why did you have me? If I had enough money, I'd have love.* He looked up at me for a moment and then back down at the floor and tapped his feet.

While growing up, David heard a clear message from his mom that they couldn't afford this anymore, or they couldn't do that anymore. She told him that they used to have more money before he was born, but now it had to go to keep him clothed, fed, and with a roof over his head. She told him they used to do lots of things they couldn't do now.

A child's mind doesn't have the logical reasoning power of an adult. Children often take things literally and personally. And then they grow up and begin to take actions over and over again consistent with the literal thoughts they formed as children.

David's clear impression from childhood was that he was a financial burden to the family and that they shouldn't have had him. He didn't hear, "I love you" or "We're so glad to have you." He never got the message, "You are our pride and joy and we will spend whatever it takes to provide the best possible life for you given our limited means."

He decided instead that if the family had had more money, then his parents would have loved him more. He formed a literal belief that he was unlovable and unwanted. He was a mistake, he shouldn't be here. He said to himself, "Hopefully, I won't be a burden for anyone else. I'll just work hard and get by."

It didn't matter how many classes he took to figure out a passion in his life or a path to a new job. None of it was going to work until he began investigating his money baggage. His money baggage subverted his capacity to earn money or find opportunities.

Your thoughts—your money baggage—will sabotage all your good intentions. David's meager life was in perfect harmony with his money baggage. It created his demeanor, it picked the clothes he wore, and it gave him the job he had. It chose his little apartment and made sure that he never dated. Deep down, David's money baggage told him that he did not deserve.

One description of why our conscious intentions around money are so often frustrated is in Neale Donald Walsch's book *Conversations with God*. Walsch says that it is our *sponsoring* thought—literally the thought behind the thought—that has the most say over our reality. It is the unconscious thought beneath the conscious one that is most responsible for the way our life is.

Your money baggage is formed by such a sponsoring thought. It formed in childhood. It became part of the foundation upon which you created your life. A belief that you do not deserve, held deeply in your subconscious, will frustrate all your attempts to bring sustained happiness into your life.

The process is faultless. If your money baggage says money is bad, you will, in perfect harmony with this belief, find a way to keep it away from you. Or if it does come, you will find a way to get it out of your hands, quickly.

When you discover your money baggage, you discover the sponsoring thought that has always been there running the show. You discover the way your money baggage directs your life by posing as the truth. It tries to convince you that it is in charge, not you. And it will continue to do so as long as you live an unexamined life around the deeper attitudes you have around money.

What conclusions and decisions did you make about money that are still silently directing your life today? The clue to discovering your money baggage might be in some behavior you have—shopping even when you don't really need what you are buying; avoiding asking your boss for a raise; always looking for bargains even if you have to drive all the way across town to get them; never buying yourself anything nice; or wearing heavy sweaters when you could turn up the heat in your apartment to a reasonable level instead.

Start to jot down all the behaviors you have that are related to money using WORKSHEET 2: MONEY IN MY ADULT YEARS. Do you resist giving money to charity? Is it hard for you to not take advantage of a sale even when you don't really need what you are buying? Is it hard to say no to your children when they want you to buy them something? Take these behaviors as clues and ask yourself why you are doing them and what early experiences might be influencing you. The answer will lead you to your money baggage.

Let's take a deeper look at how money baggage affects every part of our lives by focusing in on four of the main areas: relationships, work, finances, and family.

~

CHAPTER 5

MONEY BAGGAGE AND RELATIONSHIPS

*M*oney affects every aspect of our lives, and therefore has a profound effect on our intimate relationships. Few people will disagree with me when I say that money is a common reason for many arguments. Survey after survey shows this. Money, in fact, is often cited as the number one reason people get divorced.

Our money baggage influences everything: whether we can find a partner, whom we choose, how easy or difficult it is to maintain a long-term relationship, and our tendency to lay blame on our partner when discussing finances.

Recall Oliver, whose father yelled about the grocery bill. He fled Austria at age fifteen, far from the painful memories of his parents' fights over money. He became a farmer in Canada and spent most of his life avoiding having to deal with money. His money baggage is: *We don't have the money, something is always wrong! I'm out of here!*

Oliver had accountants deal with the farm finances, and he let his wife, Anita, handle the family money. Anita's money baggage is: *I'm bad with money and the end is always near.* She shared:

I have wanted money—and what money can provide—ever since I heard the alluring sound of my grandfather's coins jingling in his pocket when I was very small, signaling he wanted to give them to me. Money was good stuff; magical and mysterious and good things came from having it.

But Mom thought it wasn't proper for me to want money and ask people for it. So after being allowed, once, to have Grandpa's coins, it was "No!" after that.

One day Anita took some coins off her dad's dresser and was punished for it. She was locked in her bedroom and not allowed to come out until she confessed and apologized to her father. She refused to admit having taken the money, even though everyone knew she had. She cried and cried but her parents would not let her come out of her room. She felt afraid and ashamed. Her conclusion about money was that she was bad with it and that she couldn't be trusted.

As an adult, Anita reinforced her subconscious belief that she was bad with money by marrying Oliver, who she knew would be a good provider. She also became a compulsive spender. So here you have a compulsive spender, who believes deep down she is bad with money, in charge of the family finances, married to someone who wants to avoid dealing with money altogether. Arguments about money were commonplace in their marriage.

OLIVER: Anita handled the household money, a bookkeeper handled the farm bills, and an accountant prepared the year-end financials. I, on the other hand, would take the garbage out, sweep the floor, clean up the office, and file paperwork before starting on a budget. A budget that should only take two days to do would take me two to three weeks to finish.

ANITA: I always enjoyed going shopping—until it was time to think about coming home, and then apprehension set in. I dreaded having to face the music and having Oliver find out I'd been shopping again. As the guilt took over, I would subtly maneuver my parcels from the trunk to the house to my closet unnoticed. I would be scared wearing the new clothes or using the new appliance for the first time, just waiting for Oliver to ask if it was new.

OLIVER: I never wanted to know what she bought. Our money was her responsibility anyway. I'd think, "When the money is gone, she can't spend anymore." Well, that was a wrong assumption, but it was fine as long as I didn't have to deal with it. Secretly, I could blame my financial ruin on her reckless and unappreciative spending.

ANITA: My spending contributed to many fights in our marriage. When it came time to look at our finances, especially if I said we needed more money, we might as well have been reading from scripts, as we both said the exact same things every time. He'd say, "If you didn't spend so much we'd have enough." "Well," I'd say, "if you would just get involved in knowing where our money goes. Groceries just keep going up, the kids need braces. We do have a joint checking account—you could look at that from time to time. And if you could get the farm bills under control, we'd be fine." These fights never stopped me from spending for long and it never stopped Oliver from avoiding money. For twenty-five years we were talking about money—but we never heard a word the other said. It looked like a wonderful marriage to the outside world, but it wasn't.

A lot of money disagreements arise out of our partner's fears and automatic behaviors colliding with our own. A subtle dance often ensues to avoid dealing with it, while frustration and resentment grow. Most of the time, one spouse blames the other and just can't understand why the other one won't change his or her behavior.

How often have you said to yourself, "If only my partner would handle money the way I do, or do as I say, then our money problems would be over!" All the while your spouse is thinking, "If only my spouse would handle money the way I do—*then* our money problems would be over!"

For most of us, it was common to grow up in a household where money was not discussed. Often couples tell me they seldom or never talk about money, even those who have been together for decades. It's simply taboo. Given that money is so central to every decision we make, how can we have an honest and fulfilling relationship if we do not talk about it? And how can we talk about it if we don't understand our money baggage and how it is driving our own behavior?

Are you in a relationship where money is not discussed? How come? What are you afraid of? What is your partner afraid of? Help each other discover your respective money baggage. What behavior do you notice in yourself and your partner? Explore where these behaviors came from.

You might save each other a lot of suffering. You might begin to let go of old patterns that don't serve your soul and become closer as a couple; it might even save your marriage.

For some couples, money baggage does not always lead to arguments. In a household of relative harmony, however, it can still play a powerful role. It can create a separateness that does not allow for complete emotional connection in the relationship.

Here is the story of Ellen, an independent woman. Ellen's money baggage is: *I have to do everything all by myself, and I've got to work really hard to get money.*

⸺

When I was six years old I wanted to buy some candy or a toy. I asked my dad if he'd give me some money and he replied, in his deep voice with his arms crossed in front of him, "Well, I can't just give it to you. You're going to have to work for it."

I said that I would wash the car. He agreed and away I went.

I pulled the hose across the front yard, got a bucket of warm soapy water and some rags, and proceeded to scrub and soap and wash the car. What a sight that car was to behold! All shiny and clean. It was beautiful and I had done it all myself.

I ran inside to tell dad and collect my reward. He said, "Well, I've got to inspect the car before I can give you the money." So I nervously followed him outside and watched him walk around the car looking here and there, sighing, and nodding to himself. Finally, he pointed out that I missed the lower part on the car door. I bravely listened as he told me I had to clean that first before he'd pay me.

So he left and I proceeded to scrub that part and check all the other parts of the car. I called him again and this time he pointed out the hubcaps. They had spokes and he told me I needed to use a toothbrush on them. So I choked back the tears and cleaned the hubcaps.

The next time it was car's roof. I had only hosed it down, because I was too short to reach it. So I had to get a chair and wash it with soap. My dad left and I started crying.

I can't remember how many times we went through this but eventually he laughed at me as he pulled a quarter out of his pocket and gave it to me.

—

Ellen's dad might very well have been trying to teach her the values of working hard and doing a complete job. But he forgot he was dealing with a sensitive six-year-old girl and it was the first time she had ever worked for money.

It's no surprise she grew up to be a workaholic and a perfectionist. She also vowed not to ever let anyone lord over her with money. She became very successful and an "independent woman." That sounds good on the surface, but it arose from a deep underlying belief that people with power and money will humiliate and control you. So she set out to make sure that never happened. She was determined she would earn what she needed and rise above the need to ask anyone for money.

She did eventually marry, but even within the relationship she held on to her independence, in one case insisting that she save up for her own maternity leave instead of letting her husband help out. She always had to do it herself because her money baggage would not let her trust anyone else with her fate as it related to money, especially not a man. They did not fight about money, but her money baggage created an emotional gulf that prevented a true partnership.

How is money handled in your relationship? Who pays the bills? Have you ever deferred your own career choice in the interest of your partner's? Do you feel as if you have to rely on another person for money or that you can't rely on anyone but yourself? Do you argue about money? Is money misused as a source of power in your relationship? Does the person who makes the most money typically make the decisions? Ask yourself why these patterns exist.

Sit down with your partner and discuss your money issues with each other. Ask if there is any fear about money. Share your own fears. Discover your money baggage together and see how each other's money baggage creeps into and affects your relationship.

CHAPTER 6

~

MONEY BAGGAGE AND WORK

We design our work lives around our money baggage without realizing it. Perhaps you are working below your true abilities or are in a job that pays a lower wage than you deserve. Maybe you are working long hours at a job you don't like. Your money baggage is the culprit behind these patterns. Until you find out what it is, it will be as if an invisible force field is keeping you in your current circumstances.

Roger, a participant at one of my workshops, was typical of many people who know what they want to do but stay glued to their unsatisfying job. Roger was a marketing executive: crisp suit, starched white shirt, talking to everyone around him before the class started, confident, smooth, well-liked.

At the beginning of class I always ask, "Why are you here? What do you want to accomplish by being here?" The first words out of Roger's mouth were, "I hate my job. I hate marketing; I can't do it any more. I make a ton of money but it's killing me."

I asked him what he would do if he weren't doing marketing. He didn't have to think for even a second. "I'd be a teacher. I'd love to teach math. But I'd only make a third of what I make now."

"Well, could you possibly support yourself on a teacher's salary?"

"I don't know, I don't have any debt," he said. "I do have a lot in the stock market. I never really considered it."

As Roger was growing up his mom told him repeatedly, "You are only as good as the amount of money you make. If you have money; you are a better person." Roger's uncle worked as a brakeman for the railroad. His mom told him, "You don't want to turn out to be like Uncle Fred." The fact is, Roger admired his uncle, who had a huge heart, played guitar, was fun to be around, and taught Roger a lot of great things. But his mom made it clear: Roger needed to rise above any occupation that seemed blue collar or ordinary.

Other times his mom would say, "See that person? He's a social worker. It's too bad. He doesn't make much money. You can do more for the world if you have money." Roger's money baggage was clear: *Money determines my self-worth.*

He got a business degree and, as soon as he graduated from college, went for a job that would make him a lot of money—marketing for a pharmaceutical company. And he was very successful.

"So your lifestyle might allow you to become a teacher," I said, "if you took a hard look at it. But you dread having the conversation with your mom, telling her you have decided to follow your heart? Is that it?"

"No," Roger said. "Mom's been dead for ten years." I was stunned. Ten years, but he still heard her voice in his ear, keeping him from pursuing his passion to teach. That is how powerful our money baggage is. As long as we don't examine it to find out why we make the decisions about money that we do, we will be frustrated in our attempts to follow our hearts.

Our money baggage not only keeps us from pursuing work we love; it also can keep us in lower-paying jobs than we deserve. Virginia, one of my clients, runs the information technology department at a state agency.

Virginia is exceptional at her job. She keeps up with the latest technological advancements and she is constantly expected to do miraculous things with few resources. On call twenty-four hours a day, she is the one who has to fix things if the system crashes or malfunctions. She only gets called when there is a problem—and when there is, it always needs to be fixed right away. She has worked at the agency for twenty-one years. In six more years she can retire. But the job is wearing her out.

One irony about her situation is that she works within driving distance of many software companies starved for skilled workers. Often she trains someone who then gets hired away at a starting salary far exceeding hers. She could easily triple her income and work shorter hours at a private company.

I told her, "Quit! Get out! Who cares?" Based on the retirement projection for her and her husband (who makes pretty good money as a mid-level bank manager), she really doesn't need to make a lot of money, maybe $40,000 a year. "Do you know how many jobs there are in the world paying $40,000–$50,000 that you are completely qualified for? Even if you didn't have the right skills, you could get them in a relatively short time." The more I asked her why she stayed and why she didn't go get another job, the more she fidgeted in her seat.

My logic fell on deaf ears because her money baggage is: *I can't risk—the world can't be trusted.* Her father was an entrepreneur who made lots of money but went broke again and again. The family was always in upheaval. "It's our lot in life, honey," her mom would say.

To Virginia, taking a risk in her life called up the uncertainty of her childhood, going from boom to bust and back again. Despite all the possibilities before her, she loved the security of her current job and she was unwilling to go beyond her comfort zone. Her money baggage told her that if she took risks, she'd probably get hurt. She would rather suffer than explore the options available to her.

But she couldn't realize any of this until she uncovered her money baggage. Then it became clear to her why she was clinging to a painful dead-end job.

The world is full of talented people working at jobs below their abilities. They stay in professions that don't pay very much money or that they don't like. They believe that staying safe is better than leaving, even if staying is painful.

I don't believe our souls buy into this idea that stagnation is a safe place. I think our soul wants us to grow. I believe our soul wants us to find our own unique gift. To find work that expresses who we really are, what our true passions are.

Ask yourself if you love your job. If you don't love it, why are you still doing it? Why aren't you moving on? Do you deserve a raise or more time off and are afraid to ask for it? Do you tell yourself that the reason you work so hard is that you have to support your family? Do you take lunch breaks? Do you take all the vacation time you have earned? The answers to these questions are pointing you toward your money baggage.

It might be useful to list every job you've ever had and see if you can find a recurring theme. Were you following your deepest interests and your heart? Were you paid what you were worth? What types of bosses did you have? Take this information and use it to better understand your money baggage, and become more conscious of its influence in your life, especially at work.

CHAPTER 7

~

MONEY BAGGAGE AND FINANCES

$\mathcal{O}$ur money baggage affects our financial life more directly than any other area. One dramatic story that illustrates this is that of Paul, a real estate investor. His experience in childhood led to millions of dollars in losses and also to alcoholism, drug abuse, and broken marriages.

As a child, Paul's dad rarely spoke to him or spent much time with him. In Paul's eyes his dad was powerful, large, and remote. When Paul was five years old, his dad gave him money to go to the corner store for a quart of milk. He never remembered his dad trusting him before, especially with money. To Paul this was a chance to shine in his dad's eyes. He felt he was setting out on the most important mission of his life.

Paul bought the milk, got the change, and set off at a run for home. On the way back he got distracted by an anthill, and played around a small creek tossing in a few rocks. When he got home, he proudly gave the milk to his dad. His dad, barely looking up from the TV, asked him for the change. Paul dug in his front pocket, but the change was gone. He searched his other pockets to no avail and a wave of panic set in.

His dad got angry and asked him if he had hidden the money for himself. Paul denied it and started to get "real scared." His dad made him go back to the store and look for the change. He spent the next hour, almost paralyzed by fear, retracing his steps to and from the store, but found nothing.

He felt like a failure, and was sick to his stomach when he admitted defeat to his dad. Paul remembers to this day how angry his dad got, glaring at him, his lips drawn together. Without a word, he walked out of the room leaving Paul alone, and didn't speak to him for the rest of the day. His dad never trusted him with money again.

At the workshop thirty-six years later, Paul identified his money baggage for the first time: *"No matter what happens, I'm just going to lose it anyway."*

Even by age seven Paul had become a hard worker and habitual spender, and had his own bank account. When it got up to eight dollars, he withdrew it and had an older kid buy cigarettes with it.

He remembers buying school lunches in high school for his friends so he wouldn't have to keep money in his pocket, all the while not consciously remembering the event of losing the milk money or being aware of why he felt compelled to spend everything he got. He became student body president and an all-star football player, but slowly grew apathetic. Deep down he felt he was a failure. "So what does a failure do?" he asked himself. "A failure screws up." He often found himself without two cents to his name. Any time he had some success, he knew it wouldn't last.

He had a naturally entrepreneurial nature and made a lot of money, but he spent it on partying. He started drinking a lot and became an alcoholic. He got into real estate and made a ton of money. Then he'd take two or three years off, living "the good life." Tropical islands, large yachts, villas, wine, women, and song. He could never accumulate anything. He had to spend it all.

He got divorced twice and never formed lasting friendships. Who would want to be friends with such a failure? He was foreclosed on three times and went bankrupt twice. Millions of dollars "went through my pockets," as he put it.

You might read Paul's story and say, how silly. How silly that a simple little event in childhood like losing money on the way back from the store can so influence a life. Well, our money baggage is often silly—from an adult point of view. But it is not the adult who is in charge of issues with money; it is the child-mind in action inside the adult. A child's mind is extremely impressionable; it believes things with great conviction, and it never forgets.

This single event of buying some milk and then losing the change crystallized, in Paul's young mind, a deep belief about himself, and it was backed up by many years of experience. His conclusion that he was a failure arose from his decision that he did not live up to his father's expectations. In a similar way, we form our internal stories *(No matter what happens, I'm just going to lose it anyway.)* and then externalize them to make our stories come true in the world.

Some people worry about money a lot. Even when they have plenty, or have the promise of plenty in the future, they never feel they have enough. If they do have enough, they spend it. By spending it, they perpetuate the feeling of not having enough. Other people sabotage their own dreams just as they begin to succeed, because they believe so deeply and unconsciously that success would ruin their life. This becomes their money baggage. They will talk a lot about wanting to succeed and sincerely try to make it come true, but as long as their money baggage is in charge, success will be fleeting.

This entire mechanism occurs automatically. People don't do these things on purpose. They are not aware of why they go on spending sprees, running up large credit card debts, or why they can't earn more than they do, or why they constantly bounce checks.

Some people use "retail therapy" to avoid their painful issues around money. By spending, they distract themselves from having to investigate this pain. I see other people who cannot spend money on themselves because they don't believe they are worthy.

Look to your behaviors around money and your current financial situation. Don't assume these behaviors and the state of your finances are normal and just "the way it is." Question them. Ask yourself why you do the things you do in your life with money. Do you hoard it? Do you find yourself in constant debt? Are you unable to set clear limits for your children when it comes to spending? Are you always thinking you need more? Do you neglect yourself—wear second-hand clothes and never get around to treating yourself with something nice?

By answering these questions you will get below the surface of your habitual thoughts about money and to the root cause of your behaviors. By understanding the cause you can begin to take steps to create new thoughts to better shape your life and your relationship to money, especially when it comes to your personal finances.

CHAPTER 8

MONEY BAGGAGE AND FAMILY

One of the most painful aspects of money baggage is the effect it has on those we love the most. Wendell's story illustrates this. His money baggage is: *Money is more important than family.*

When I was five years old, my father decided to go into business for himself. We moved to Hanover, Pennsylvania after he purchased an Oldsmobile/Cadillac dealership.

He was gone a lot. Out the door at eight o'clock every morning, he would return for dinner around six, and then go back to work, not coming home until after my sister, brother, and I had gone to bed. I don't remember him ever reading us any books or tucking me into bed at night. When

I was eight years old, I joined a Little League baseball team. My dad never came to a game.

To spend time with my father, I would go to work with him and we would have breakfast together at the Sunnyside Diner, the greasy spoon behind the dealership.

When I was ten, I began to play racquetball on a regular basis with a friend down the street. I came up with an idea: if I worked really hard to earn some money mowing lawns in the summer and shoveling snow in the winter, I could give my dad a racquetball racquet. *Then* we could spend time together playing racquetball.

I never felt more proud than on that Christmas, watching my dad unwrap the new racquet I had bought with my own $15. We talked about playing together the next week, but he never had time. So we talked about getting in a game after the first of the year, then maybe in the spring. It never happened; the dealership always came first, second, and third. My dad never once used that racquet.

So, I spent a lot of Saturdays around the dealership, washing cars. I'd do anything to be with him. My wife still wonders to this day why I can't stand to wash our cars.

Wendell remembers his father fondly. His dad didn't intentionally ignore him—Wendell knows this; his father was simply living a life consistent with his *own* money baggage, which was to work hard, be successful, and take care of the family financially. His dad never said money was more important than family, but actions speak louder than words, and Wendell came to that conclusion on his own.

As an adult, Wendell didn't consciously believe that money was more important than family. But he took it as a fact that what a father does is work hard to make sure the family is well taken care of.

At his first job after he was married—selling cars—Wendell worked sixty-five to seventy hours a week. Some days he'd leave the house at five a.m., work all day, and get back home around seven p.m.

Just before his first son was born, Wendell went back to college for an accounting degree and afterwards started working sixty-five to seventy hours a week as a CPA. He began to travel internationally, with a goal to become a partner at a large accounting firm. One day, flying back from Europe, Wendell started to reflect on his life.

———

I began to wonder if all the time away from my family was worth it. I suddenly realized that I had missed out on more than ten years of putting my boys to bed, of having dinner with my family, of attending my sons' sporting and school events. Ten years, all because I had placed work in front of my family, just as my own dad had.

I looked back across many generations of my family and saw that the same message about work had always been there: *Money is more important than family.* I became determined on the flight home to break this painful cycle. I wanted to make it up to my kids and wife before it was too late.

Be assured that, to the extent our money baggage is unexamined, we are passing it on to our kids. You might never even talk about money around them, but your kids are like little scientists watching and picking up clues and drawing conclusions. They watch how you approach work, how you talk about it, and how you deal with money. If you are working at a job you don't like, they take that in. If they see you and your spouse fight about money, they make note of it. They notice when you don't have time for them. They will assume that whatever you choose to do instead of spending time with them is more important to you than they are, especially if you don't consciously understand and explain the reasons why. From their observations of your behaviors, conclusions about life and money silently take shape in their young minds.

Parents who work too much often feel guilty and try to compensate for it by giving their kids the best. They provide a nice house, give them plenty of things, and send them to good schools. But they aren't giving their kids what the kids really want: emotional connection and time together. The parents might alleviate their guilt by giving presents or money to show their love, but that can lead kids to conclude that money equals love. A lot of people's money baggage forms around this confusion.

When they grow up, they might emulate their folks, working hard, being too busy, and giving their own kids presents and money to show them that they love them. And the cycle continues.

People arrive at the workshops I lead unaware of the pain they are carrying around. June, a woman in her mid-fifties, vaguely agreed with me that money was a source of suffering in her life, but she couldn't really put her finger on why.

I began talking about how our money baggage comes from a decision we make when we are young. Suddenly tears were running down June's cheeks. When I asked her if she knew what her money baggage was, she said: *Money will destroy your life and relationships, so pretend it is not there.*

"My grandmother had a lot of money," she said, her voice cracking a bit. "She basically controlled the family with it. What happened in my family is exactly what *Grandma* wanted to happen. If she gave you money for college, you went to a college that met her approval. If she gave you a down payment on a house, it had to be a house she liked."

June saw her Grandma destroy the family; she had her hooks in just about everything from financing the house to setting up college funds for the kids. When Grandma didn't get what she wanted, she went on a rampage. June's parents always caved in.

The older Grandma got, the more demands she made, and the more irrational the demands became. If someone disobeyed her, he or she was uninvited to family gatherings, cut out of the will, and essentially disowned.

June's brother decided to go overseas to study. This appalled his grandmother. She believed he should first go to an Ivy League school and later could "prance around the world." He followed his heart instead and Grandma did not spare him her wrath.

June remembered sitting down at Christmas dinner at her grandmother's the following year, the long table arrayed with china and crystal. It all looked elegant and perfect. But there was a huge hole, the empty chair where her brother usually sat. It was understood that no one should even mention his name.

Grandma cashed in the college fund she had set up for June's brother. June loved him and was deeply disappointed when she saw her family not say a thing about it for fear Grandma would take something away from them.

When the grandmother died, she left a considerable sum to June in a trust fund. June pretended it was not there. She didn't want to deal with it, so she had accountants deal with it. She really didn't know consciously why, but her money baggage was telling her, "If I touch it, it will destroy my life. It will destroy my family. I'll be like Grandma."

By unearthing her money baggage, June saw for the first time how much and for how long she had silently suffered around money. She saw how her beliefs had affected her own family—that money was bad, that it was an instrument that people used to control others and inflict pain, and that money was something to be avoided at all cost.

Is it time to break the painful cycles in your life? Look at how the messages you learned about money as a child affected your family then, and how those attitudes influence your family now. What are the messages you overtly or covertly give to your kids? Ask your kids what they are learning from you about money. Go back to your childhood and get clear about your own money baggage. You owe it to yourself and to your loved ones.

~

CHAPTER 9

MONEY BAGGAGE PRINCIPLE #3:
OUR MONEY BAGGAGE IS NOT TRUE

*T*here is a universal truth about your money baggage: it is not true. It is not true that you do not deserve money. It is not true that money is bad or that you have to work hard for it. Money doesn't necessarily corrupt and people with money and power will not necessarily humiliate and control you. It is not true that a woman cannot be powerful and competent with money. It's not true that you can't follow your heart and earn a good living at the same time. Your money baggage only seems true to you because you have made it so inside your head.

Money baggage always speaks in the language of limitation:
Without money, I have no value.
It's selfish and greedy to want.

I have to take care of myself.
I have to be useful or I have no right to be here.
I have to work hard, hard, hard, or I will fail.
I will be a failure if I am not as successful as my father.
You get money not by following your spirit or doing what you want,
    but by being responsible and doing what others tell you to do.
It's not okay to spend money on myself.
I had better save because I can't depend on anything or anyone.
I'm not worth anything because I didn't earn it myself.
Money equals self-esteem.

None of these statements is inherently true. And yet we live entire lives assuming they are, doing irrational things with money that seem completely rational to us.

Gordon is someone who has received more inheritances than anyone I know. I was always a bit envious, as I often used to fantasize about getting an inheritance. Like people who fantasize about winning the lottery, I imagined what I would do with all my fantasy-inherited money.

Gordon had a unique solution for what to do with his: he gave it all away, every time. When he got an inheritance, he would proudly tell me what he had done. "Oh, my friend had some credit card debt so I paid that off." Another time he told me, "A great kid in my neighborhood wanted to go to college and didn't have the money so I gave it to him." One time it was, "This woman who works in my department really wanted to go buy this piece of land that had been in her family for many years, so I helped her with the down payment."

Within months of any inheritance, Gordon was back where he was before, working in a job he didn't really like all that much. He justified it to me by the fact that he "had to work." And then he would complain to me about how many more years he had until retirement.

I was always astounded by his generosity. I wasn't sure I could be that generous under the same circumstances. Yet, something was wrong with the picture. I always wondered why he didn't keep some of it and leave the job he didn't like. Even if he couldn't retire, he could at least use it to support a career change that would be more fulfilling to him.

Once I learned about his childhood, I came to see that giving away his inheritances wasn't just about being generous. It was also propelled by an underlying belief that money is bad.

His father, a longshoreman in Texas, had come upon sudden wealth. He had inherited a few acres of land, beneath which happened to be a lot of oil.

Most of us are unprepared for sudden wealth and his dad was no exception. What had been a fairly happy existence for Gordon ended. His father bought a large yacht, quit working, and over time became a bit of a local playboy and carouser. A young mistress entered the picture, a divorce followed, and the family was torn apart.

It was clear to Gordon that money destroys family. His money baggage became: *Money is bad; it corrupts.*

Gordon got rid of his inheritances in seemingly honorable ways. He gave it to people who really appreciated it, or who really needed it. It seemed very virtuous. But his generosity really stemmed from the fact that he had a deep fear that money would corrupt him.

As obvious as it might seem to an outside observer, Gordon had never made the connection between his altruistic pattern of giving away money and his dad's behaviors. His early painful imprinting—his money baggage—was running the show, keeping him in a steady low-paying job that he disliked. He was controlled by the fear that money might tear apart his own family and life.

Of course it isn't true that money is necessarily bad or that it corrupts, but Gordon believed it was. As children, we live in a world defined by our money baggage, a decision based on a misperception of reality. A single event can define our money baggage. But oftentimes, our money baggage develops over many years. It can arise and be reinforced over decades from a mood in the home or a parent's recurrent attitude. It may not be obvious until we begin to look at its effect on our adult lives.

Our money baggage might work for us for a while. But when we are adults, it stops working, and we can find ourselves living dysfunctional, frustrating, and fearful lives. When we find ourselves in jobs we do not like; when we are unable to find work; when we cannot hold onto money or make enough to support our dreams; or when we attempt to improve our lives but are frustrated at every turn—all these situations revolve around our money baggage.

Money is involved in all aspects of our lives, and when we decide to work on our money issues, we find a powerful access point to multiple aspects of ourselves, an access point that helps bring to consciousness that which is unconscious. It's the first step in healing emotional pain and finding our soul's work. It all begins with the realization that our money baggage isn't true.

—

CHAPTER 10

TAKING THE JOURNEY:
EXERCISES FOR DISCOVERING YOUR MONEY BAGGAGE

*J*oseph Campbell's landmark book *The Hero with a Thousand Faces* presents a compelling case: that at the heart of all world cultures lives one primary story—the journey of the Hero. The Hero journeys from the ordinary world to the underworld and then re-emerges with a gift for mankind.

Similarly, on the journey to discover your money baggage, you must first go down into the underworld of your past to that which is unconscious. Then, when you emerge, you can form a more conscious and fulfilling relationship to money. It is a journey of heroic proportions, a sacred journey.

This journey takes us from our ordinary world, where money is a source of suffering, to an extraordinary world, where money is aligned with and empowers our soul's calling. It is a journey from unconsciousness to consciousness, from fear to love, from artificial control to true inner power. It is Dorothy's journey to Oz, leaving behind the bleak black-and-white world of Kansas and exploring a new world of color and adventure and potential, only this new world is real and you want to stay.

To decide to examine your life and become consciously aware of your pain in relation to money is to begin your soul's journey. Because money infiltrates everything we do, it is a journey that involves the entirety of your being. When we begin the journey to transform our relationship to money, we begin to rethink everything in our lives.

The moment you decide to discover your money baggage is the moment you go from bobbing on the surface of the ocean to diving down to explore the depths. Those things that hold us back, all our fears and habitual responses to life, lurk below the surface. Healing is the process of bringing these patterns up to the surface and into the light.

If you have read this far, you've already begun your journey. To recap and give you more structure to the process, I suggest you do the following exercises, using the worksheets in the Appendix to help solidify your understanding of your own money baggage.

YOUR PERSONAL MONEY HISTORY. In Worksheet 1: Money in My Younger Years, explore your history with money by writing down your childhood thoughts and memories about money. Reflect upon your earliest experiences with money. In those memories you will find two things: a blueprint for the ways you have formed your current life, and the reasons behind the specific struggles you have regarding money. In Worksheet 2: Money in My Adult Years, examine how you currently relate to money to see how thoroughly your early imprinting has defined your adult world. What these two worksheets reveal will lead you to your money baggage.

YOUR PERSONAL MONEY BAGGAGE. Using Worksheet 3: Discovering My Money Baggage, write down your own personal money baggage. Don't worry about whether you get it right or wrong. First consider the stories in this book, do the exercise above, and then trust the process. Your money baggage will emerge, and when it does, write it down, and then look at it in relationship to the various areas of your life listed at the bottom of the worksheet.

ASK SOMEONE CLOSE TO YOU. If you are having trouble determining your money baggage, ask your spouse, partner, or good friend what they think your money baggage is. You will be amazed how clearly others see you. Use this dialog to help you discover your money baggage and don't be defensive. Be open to hearing what the other person has to say.

WRITE, WRITE, WRITE. Journaling can be a great way to trigger memories. Some of you may need to write out your entire life story to get to your money baggage, or write about specific money memories in detail before you can distill this information down to one simple money baggage statement. It may be helpful to write a longer version that you can then condense. Here is one man's version of that process:

—

MONEY BAGGAGE: I'm not good enough on my own. If I shine or speak up, I'll get rejected, hurt, and overpowered. I can't be myself and have money or success. I have to hide, lay low, do what you want me to do. Be responsible. I'm not supposed to talk about money. It's a secret.

CONDENSED: I'm not good enough on my own. I can't be myself and have money.

—

Condensing your statement will help you really capture the essence of your money baggage. You should express it in a child's language, in the simplest words you can. There may be several threads—

different variations on the theme that you come up with—but ultimately, there is one, maybe two core beliefs that you believe to be true. Distill these down to their simplest form.

You will know you have your money baggage if, when you say it out loud, it catches a bit in your throat. It can be embarrassing. It brings up emotions that have been deeply hidden. It might even make you feel a bit queasy.

Once you've done the work, you should have a pretty good idea of what your own bleak personal "Kansas" is. Do you think counting chickens comes before family or fun? Do you believe people who have money are like Miss Gulch? Does thinking about your money baggage make you feel like the cowardly lion? Are there flying monkeys keeping you up at night worrying about money?

On your journey, you should expect to encounter obstacles, fears, tests, and disappointments. This is the juicy and interesting work of discovering yourself. And it can be a little frightening. But keep going. When you start to see the emotional baggage you have been carrying, you are beginning to care for your soul.

By drawing back the curtain you have exposed your false belief for the imposter it is. Now you are ready to articulate your new money message. You have brought your money baggage to consciousness; now it's time to set that burden down and create the rest of your life.

PART II
NEW MONEY MESSAGE

CHAPTER 11

~

WHAT'S A NEW MONEY MESSAGE?

*I*n Part I, we thoroughly explored the power that one erroneous, defining decision—our money baggage—had on the development and expression of who we are and the life we created. How, gradually, that decision determined our actions, and those actions became the core reality around which our world shaped itself.

A *new money message* is the antidote to money baggage. It is the process of generating and activating a new language inside ourselves. It is a conscious infusion of the soul's desire, a focal point in the form of a statement that we allow to guide our choices for the rest of our lives.

It all begins with our thoughts, which become our words, and then our actions.

The words we think and say to ourselves influence our lives profoundly. Our world conforms to these words. One of my friend's daughters who is somewhat gifted in math uses her words and thoughts in a way that strongly influences her life. When asked what her favorite subject is, she replies, "I love math. I'm really good at it." This response helps cultivate an attitude of curiosity and self-confidence, eagerness, and self-assuredness with regard to math. She approaches her homework and tests with the confidence that she can figure it out. Her actions are consistent with her deepest self, and her world gradually shapes itself to those actions.

Compare this to the woman who, as a child, was also good at math but who didn't study for a test and failed it. When her teacher made a comment about the test being one that should be easy to pass, the student started doubting her math abilities, and gradually decided she just wasn't good at math. Now, as an adult, she doesn't balance her checkbook, freezes when it comes to reviewing loan documents, and procrastinates on paying her bills—all because her money baggage says she's not good at math.

Our money baggage is about the past, and yet it defines our present circumstances and attitudes about money; it speaks in the language of fear and contraction. It comes from a forgotten place in childhood and has lodged itself in our subconscious.

Our new money message is about the world we will create; it speaks in the language of love and expansion. It is formed consciously in adulthood and will transform our subconscious and ultimately our outer life. It expresses itself from our soul.

When we create our money message we are generating and activating a new language inside ourselves. Our new money message is a fresh centering point. It is the energy that will shape and empower the rest of our lives.

Just as we formed a decision about money early on and then lived our lives in alignment with that decision, we can now create a new decision, a new thought—this time more consciously—and align our lives with it. If we take actions consistent with this new thought—our money message—our lives will never be the same.

~

CHAPTER 12

I DISCOVER MY NEW MONEY MESSAGE

*F*or more than thirty years I operated from a limiting belief system. My money baggage, *You have to work hard to make money, and even if you do, you'll never make enough,* was an unconscious but powerful force that took control of my life. When I began to examine it and see the impact it had on my life, I was stunned. How could something as simple as one thought have such a pervasive influence on my entire life?

Yet it was true: my life was in perfect correlation with a thought I had thought and acted on—my money baggage—thousands of times. Just a *thought*—a powerful one, an unconscious one, a life-shaping one—but still, just a *thought.*

Then it dawned on me—*I can change that thought.* Since my life was in perfect correlation with my old thought—working hard and not having enough—what if I made up a new thought? What if my actions then correlated with that new thought? How would it alter my life? What would I do with a new thought directing me? The questions started coming fast and furious. Could it be possible to not work so hard? Did I dare to dream of having more than "enough"? And if I had more than enough, what would I do with my time and money? What difference would I make in the world? And could I finally have a sense of peace and tranquility with money?

I could feel my excitement building. What if my new thought was about abundance instead of limitation? Of making a difference in the world instead of just getting by? And what if my new thought had nothing to do with working hard—imagine!

I could barely comprehend the questions; much less picture what my life could be like. Up until that moment I had known no other way to live. I could feel that these questions were stirring something deep inside me. I was determined to live my life differently—to care for my soul. I didn't know if it would work. But I felt a growing determination to live my life more consistently with my ultimate purpose, my soul's calling. But how?

I began to deeply ponder what the new thought might be that would feel aligned with my deepest sense of self. What words might shape my life in new and exciting ways? What would be the thought, the one thought that would most deeply care for my soul? I worked on it for many days. I was quiet and listened to what my soul was saying. Each day I spent time gazing out the window across the vista to the mountains in the distance. I watched the wind move through the trees and let it calm me. I began to really hear what my soul was calling me to do.

Eventually these words came to me and I wrote them down: *It is my birthright to have abundance in all areas of my life and I give generously from this abundance.* It felt like it came from the deepest part of my being.

It called to me, yet it simultaneously felt very strange to even *think* this new, outrageous thought, much less entertain the idea of actually saying it out loud. And forget about telling anyone else— that was out of the question. How could this "poor farm girl" from Colorado be so audacious as to think her life could possibly be filled with abundance?

Yet when I said these words in my head, *It is my birthright to have abundance in all areas of my life and I give generously from this abundance,* I felt a wave of calm come over me. A feeling of relief— finally the grip of working hard was dissipating. The tension, the fear, the anxiety was dissolving. And in its place came excitement, a sense of freedom, and the slightest glimmer of new possibilities. I started to feel centered, at peace. At last I could see the faintest outline of a new life full of hope and contribution.

I began by taking new actions. I started to take baby steps in line with my new money message. At first I started going home at 6 p.m. instead of 7 p.m. I noticed my business didn't fall apart. What really needed to get done got done.

And then I began to ask myself what else I could do to live my life in accordance with this new money message. I continued to leave work at a reasonable hour. I made sure I had fun on weekends and spent time with my family. I hired other people to do some of the work for me. I began to make bigger and bigger contributions to causes I believed in.

Whenever I fell into my old automatic behavior about money, I would catch myself and then get my thinking and actions back on track with my new money message. It didn't happen overnight. And my old thoughts—my fear-based thoughts—came back frequently. I had lived unconsciously inside of my money baggage for most of my life. It was going to take a bit of diligence, a few experiments, some risk, and a lot of faith to change that.

But over time, by persistently observing myself, I began to understand more and more deeply what was leading to different results in my life: it was that I was progressively taking actions consistent with my new money message.

Today, I work less than I ever have and my financial planning practice is successful beyond my wildest dreams. I work with a team of employees who are a joy to be around. I look forward to coming to work each day. I consider it a privilege to be in client meetings where we discuss their goals and dreams and how to achieve them financially.

My family and I take seven to eight weeks of vacation each year. I volunteer for organizations that are important to me and my family. We are blessed to be able to give money away to causes and charities we care deeply about.

The journey has been long and it is never over. I still struggle with my old money baggage from time to time, but the simple fact remains: my life changed when I changed my thought about money and then took actions aligned with this new thought.

I now know in the depths of my heart that I am doing what my soul is calling me to do—helping other people discover a new relationship to money, which influences all aspects of their lives and leads them to express what *their* soul is calling them to do.

These changes in my life all began with my willingness to take a look under the surface at my relationship with money and uncover the deep beliefs I held. By reading on, you, too, will learn how to design a new life in accord with your own new money message and begin to care for your soul.

~

CHAPTER 13

MONEY MESSAGE PRINCIPLE #1:
YOU DON'T HAVE TO REINVENT THE WHEEL

*Y*ou already know the process for transforming your life. The way you formed your money baggage and let it shape your life is the same way you'll form a new money message and use it to create a new life—you don't have to reinvent the wheel. The difference is that in working with your new money message, the process is conscious rather than unconscious. If you take actions consistent with your new thought—your money message—your life will begin to conform to possibilities you never saw before.

A thought, consciously held and reinforced by repetition and conviction, is a potent thing. It's the first part of the process of working with your new money message.

Norman Vincent Peale discusses the power of thought in his book *Positive Imaging*:

An image formed and held tenaciously in the conscious mind will pass presently, by a process of mental osmosis, into the unconscious mind. And when it is accepted firmly in the unconscious, the individual will strongly tend to have it, for then it has you. So powerful is the imaging effect on thought and performance that a long held visualization of an objective or goal can become determinative.

The next and even more important part of this process is to take actions consistent with our new money message. After creating our money message, the trick is to then apply it to our lives one step at a time. It is important to do this with the same level of conviction that we did with our money baggage, even when doubts arise. Recall that as children, and later as adults, we accepted our decisions about money as the Truth, capital T. We have to find that same level of belief and knowing for our money message to manifest and take full flower in our lives. To do so takes a kind of self-directed tenderness, an inward focus so that we become as impressionable to the messages of our soul as children are to the messages of adults.

The process begins with the creation of a new money message. Taking the time to find the right words will pay off. Ponder, revise, and fine-tune your new message until the message feels "just right." It takes courage to reflect on your life, to revive old forgotten dreams, and to assess your adult values and hopes against a changing sense of self. But when you find your new money message you will know it—it will have a sense of rightness. It may be slightly scary, but will have a feeling of great potential and possibility.

Words alone will not bring the intended results, although they are a vital part of the process. Once you have found your new money message, the process continues by identifying what steps you can take to begin to recreate your life around this new way of thinking. Focusing on our new money message brings us out of the past and into the now. From a present unconstrained by the past, we can see a new future alive with possibilities. Once we begin to take actions in harmony with our new money message, this new future begins to manifest in the present.

The process is to move from thought to word to action the way you did with your money baggage, but this time with conscious intention aligned with your new money message. Then you begin to see the results of a life moving in accord with your soul's calling.

Turn to WORKSHEET 4: CREATING MY MONEY MESSAGE in the Appendix and see if you can articulate a money message for your life that comes from your soul. If you can't find the right words yet, don't worry. Your money message will come; just keep listening.

CHAPTER 14

MONEY MESSAGE PRINCIPLE #2: LISTEN TO YOUR SOUL

*L*istening to and trusting in our soul is the most important work we have to do on earth. We were not born onto the earthly plane and then cut off from the source of life and guidance. This guidance lives in us and around us. The difficulty is that we have been conditioned away from listening to and trusting that voice deep inside us, which is the voice of our soul.

We live in a noisy world. As soon as we get up in the morning we are bombarded with opinions, others' versions of reality. They come from everywhere—the media, our spouses and families, our fellow workers.

Part of this noise is our money baggage playing over and over in our minds. When we come to the point of wanting to create a new thought to build our life around, listening is the key. Listen to your soul. Ask your soul what are its highest thoughts about money? What is it telling you to do? What is your purpose here? How can you fully express what you want to do with your life?

Oprah Winfrey modeled this process beautifully when, in a *Newsweek* article, "How I Got There," she posed these questions: "How do I accelerate my humanity? How do I use who I am on earth for a purpose that's bigger than myself? How do I align the energy of my soul with my personality and use my personality to serve my soul?"

Now comes the delicate part. You have to listen for the answer. You might hear a lot of silence at first, but that's because we are not yet tuned in to this new frequency of information. Keep listening.

Ask your soul what its highest purpose is for you. Contemplate the power of money to help make the world a better and more loving place. As words or images or feelings begin to come, write them down. This will form the nucleus of your new money message. You might start seeing yourself in a new work environment doing the work you have always dreamed of doing. You might see yourself volunteering, running for political office, pursuing a career in the arts, or quitting your job altogether and staying home with the kids. The ideas you have or the images that come to you might seem unrealistic or unattainable, but don't discount them. Write down the words that seem to fit what these images stimulate in you.

Keep in mind that the soul doesn't wear a wristwatch. So if you don't get an answer at first, don't worry; it might come to you hours or days later. It might be an incremental understanding or a sudden inspiration. You might find yourself in a conversation with someone who stimulates thoughts about a new money message. You might walk into a bookstore and find yourself pulling a book off the shelf that has your answer in it. You might have a dream that will stimulate an idea about your money message.

Oliver took the workshop twice before his new money message became clear:

—

I am kind of a meat-and-potatoes guy. My friends say I'm pretty down-to-earth. I felt funny trying to come up with my "highest thoughts" about money and my soul. But, I gave it a spin. Pretty soon some words came, so I wrote them down and I looked at them on paper: *Money is energy and I am a diesel.* As a farmer, I could relate to that. I shared it with my wife and went to bed.

I woke up in the middle of the night and I thought to myself, *Money is energy and I am the sun.* Then I immediately felt foolish. "Forget it Oliver," I told myself. "Who are you trying to kid? Don't even think of it." And I went back to sleep.

When my wife woke up the morning, she turned to me and said, "Hey Oliver, you can say, 'Money is energy and I am the sun.'"

I just about fell out of bed. I couldn't believe it. She didn't know that was the exact phrase that had come to me in the middle of the night. So, that became my new money message. It felt audacious, really. When I said *"Money is energy and I am the sun,"* I thought I was the biggest fake.

I kept repeating it and putting it out where I could see it. I had to rearrange my cells a bit but I eventually came to fully believe my money message and live my life as if it were true.

⁓

The key to discovering your money message is simply to listen and let the words arise on their own. It may not feel natural at first, but trust the process. It may take a while for your soul to realize that you are listening to it.

I want to make the point that your money message is not the *opposite* of your money baggage. You might have as your money baggage, *I am inadequate. I never measure up.* To simply revise your money baggage to its opposite—*I am adequate, I always measure up*—and have this be your money message won't work. Opposites just reinforce each other. You would be bringing up your money baggage and making it stronger by trying to push it away.

Another reason you don't want your money message to just be the opposite of your money baggage is that it probably wouldn't be big or expansive enough. It wouldn't fully encompass all the possibilities that could inspire you to new action.

Also, try not to use any words in your money message that unwittingly remind you of your money baggage. For example, if your money baggage is *Rich people are mean*, and your money message is *I will be rich and give my gift to the world*, the word "rich" may be subconsciously reminding you of your money baggage and reinforcing it. In this example, a better word to use might be "wealthy." Subtle, but that's how the subconscious works.

Lastly, don't use the words no, not, or never in your money message. Don't let any filtering or criticism or belief in scarcity come into play. You want your money message to be positive, inspiring, and free of limitations. It will help you chart a course and take you places your money baggage never could.

If someone else's money message speaks to you, by all means take it on as your own. Here is a sampling of other people's money messages from the workshops I've led:

I'm powerful and abundance is mine.

I am the empress of my financial universe.

Money is the tool and I'm a master craftsman.

My knowledge will be generously rewarded and I deserve it.

Money is my friend.

I require much that I may give much; I demand more that I may give more; I must have the best that I may give the best.

Success and family easily co-exist.

I can have it all. I deserve it totally.

Money is the natural by-product of my creative self-expression.

My money bouquet is so grand I'm challenged by what colors to display and what ones to give away.

The all-inclusive universe is safe and helpful.

I'm the gift.

Money frees my spirit to dance and sing.

I love money and money loves me, and together we play and make a difference.

The universe is an infinite, harmonious source of wisdom, wealth and prosperity. I need only listen to my soul's simple needs to be one with creation.

Money everywhere is looking for me and when it finds me, it tells its friends.

Notice that some of these examples don't even have the word money in them. That's fine. Just keep asking your soul its grandest vision of the role of money in your life and write down the words that come to you. Take time to let yourself hear your new money message. What would you like to create your most ideal life around? Don't limit yourself. Let the words come—they will come, without fail—and write them down. This will become your new money message.

Remember, the aim of creating your money message is not to become rich. It is to create a phrase or sentence that cares for your soul. Your soul is a deeper part of you, a part of you that is always there. It is like your best friend who has patiently waited all these years to have a conversation with you. By listening to what your soul is calling you to do, you have the power to transform your life. To live a life consistent with your deepest calling and passions. To have your relationship to money empower what matters most to you in the depths of your soul.

As one person who took the workshop said, "Your money baggage is a loud voice coming through the radio keeping you from hearing your soul speak to you. Your money message allows you to turn down the volume on your money baggage—and maybe even change the station."

Turn again to WORKSHEET 4: CREATING MY MONEY MESSAGE in the Appendix and write down or review your new money message.

⁓

CHAPTER 15

MONEY MESSAGE PRINCIPLE #3:
TAKE ACTIONS CONSISTENT WITH YOUR NEW MONEY MESSAGE

*A*ffirmations only work when they are supported by consistent action. Working with your new money message is not as simple as saying a new thought and sitting back to enjoy the show while your life transforms. For your money message to work it must be backed up by powerful intention, consistency, faith, and deeds.

You don't create a garden by thinking about it and affirming you have a beautiful garden. You do some planning, get your tools together, turn the soil, plant seeds, water, pull weeds, and so on.

Once you have your money message, you need to let it guide you in taking some baby steps. If your soul wants more time with your family, go home earlier. If you are an artist at heart but have never acted on it, take a class at a community college. If you hear your soul telling you that the universe is abundant and will take care of you, buy yourself a weekend at a bed-and-breakfast. If your money message tells you that you are a shining light of attraction, ask the girl behind the espresso counter, whom you've been interested in for months, out for a walk. If your money message tells you that you are a divine entrepreneur, research the new business idea you have. Meditate more. Start designing your dream house. Go in and ask the boss for a raise. Keep going. Build on your successes and don't let the failures get you down. Keep at it.

Almost everyone experiences fear at this point in the process. That means you are on the right track. The Buddhist teacher Pema Chodron says in her book *When Things Fall Apart* that "fear is a natural reaction to moving closer to the truth." It makes complete sense that committing to action elicits fear, for you have absolutely no evidence yet that your money message is true.

For most of your life, you have been influenced by your money baggage even when you didn't want to be. You may have taken actions to change your life but found yourself frustrated by the results. You may have done the ten things you were supposed to do to succeed at job interviews but still didn't get the job of your dreams.

Perhaps the reason you did not get your dream job was because you didn't know your money baggage was, and is, operating under the surface. Once you replace it with a new money message, it is time to get out in the world and experiment anew. It is time to trust, to take risks, and to believe in the wisdom of your money message.

Some people simply get paralyzed at this stage. This is another reason why it is so important to get out—shake off the paralysis, get things going, get anything moving. A misstep—and learning from it—is better than staying afraid and immobilized.

Ward learned early on that money was something you never spoke about. And you certainly never asked for it; you earned it by being "responsible." He also got the message that being responsible meant not taking risks outside the box. He developed a deep-rooted inse-curity about being himself, as he was constantly being groomed to be someone he was not. As if that weren't enough, he had an alco-holic parent, and like many children of alcoholics, he gravitated toward work that was highly structured—in his case, accounting. Creative by nature, he felt stifled by this way of life. His money bag-gage became: *I'm not good enough. I can't be myself and live.*

Ward explained, "In my family, the idea that a person could be successful and be an artist was never imagined. I never saw it as even a remote possibility until my mid-thirties." When Ward moved to Alaska "to escape the force field" of his family, he left accounting behind and instead pursued artistic adventures in theatre, photog-raphy, radio, and filmmaking. Eventually, he began an ambitious project, a feature-length documentary on girls' basketball called *The Heart of the Game*. In order to complete it, he realized, he would have to ask a lot of people for financial support. But Ward's money baggage, *I'm not good enough. I can't be myself and live*, told him that he was undeserving and that asking for money would just end in rejection. This led to an almost paralyzing fear of asking people for money for his creative projects, especially this film.

After working with me on this book, Ward's money message became: *My own deep healing love of myself radiates truth, peace, and joy into the world, which returns to me in abundant and beautifully unexpected ways*. Once he had it, he set out to apply it. He did all the necessary research to find people who might know anyone who would support his project. He met with some of them and got referrals to possible funding sources.

He decided it would be easier to ask a group than to approach an individual for money. He held a number of fundraising parties at people's homes, showed them a bit of the film, and then at the end asked the group for money. Ward shared, "It was amazing. People would pull out their checkbooks and write me $100, $250, and $500 checks. Teenagers might give me $10. I would raise somewhere between $500 and a couple of thousand dollars at each event. The more I reached out, the more I was supported."

However, he resisted seeking out major individual donors because of the fear of rejection it brought up. It took him six weeks before he called the first possible major contributor. He described sitting at his desk in an absolute spider's web of anxiety. He wrote out a little script about what he would say. And then he promised himself he would call the next day. But the next day he found half a dozen reasons why he could not call.

All the while, he kept his money message in front of him. When he did get around to his first call, the woman who answered was as nice as she could be. She agreed to meet with him the next week. When they met, she was absolutely enthused about his film and gave him $5,000 on the spot.

He still was anxious about asking people for money, but he had made an important shift in his consciousness. It was no longer about rejection or acceptance. It was about letting other people know about his humanistic intent and vision of the film and giving them an opportunity to support him.

The project went on for seven long years. He lowered his living expenses. He found a full time job making films for nonprofits and foundations, and put any extra money he earned into the film. He used up all his savings while he kept writing grants, meeting prospective donors, and looking people in the eye to ask them for support. Eventually, nearly 200 people gave him money to make his dream a reality.

His consistent, persistent actions, aligned with his money message, led to the completion of *The Heart of the Game*, which premiered at the Toronto Film Festival in 2005 and earned a distribution deal from Miramax Films. The film was shown in theaters all over the country and received rave reviews from *USA Today*; Ebert and Roeper; *O, the Oprah Magazine*; Jay Leno, and many more.

Ward and I collaborated on the writing of this book for five years. I saw firsthand the paralyzing grip Ward's money baggage had on his life. I saw him struggle to listen to his soul's calling. To find the words to create his money message. And then to find the courage to continue to take actions consistent with his money message.

There were days when we met that he was literally down to a few hundred dollars in funding for the film and he needed to raise tens of thousands more. At those moments I returned him to his money message and encouraged him to continue to take actions consistent with it. It wasn't easy. Despair and rejection took its toll. But little by little, step by step, one thing led to another and the film became a reality. A reality beyond his wildest dreams. Ward shared:

⌐

I learned so much from this process. It is hard today to even recognize the guy who, seven years ago, was afraid to ask anyone for help. I am astonished at how deeply ingrained my belief patterns were. Outwardly I may have appeared confident, but I was scared most of the time, thinking subconsciously that I didn't deserve support. I had spent most of my life living a lie about myself, and it did not go away overnight. I got counseling, I asked friends for emotional support, and though scared a lot of the time, I kept taking little steps forward. The process of transforming my old belief patterns into a new vision of myself, one that resulted in the making of my movie, has given me a quantum leap in confidence in myself and in the universe to support me.

Ward is a perfect example of how to transform old beliefs about money into a promising future. His story illustrates what is possible when the limiting bonds of one's money baggage are replaced with the limitless possibilities of a new money message. In order to create a truer life for himself, he had to first recognize the limits of his money baggage and how it ruled his life. He then created a new money message and took some action.

The most important lesson to take from Ward's story is *to keep taking actions in alignment with your new vision even when you are afraid*. It took many years but now he is living that new vision. He gave the world a gift in the form of the story of his movie and Ward's life will never be the same. He told me the other day, "I'm already half way through life but I feel this great sense of promise about the future."

My sharing all these stories is an attempt to get you to recognize some of the limiting beliefs you carry, and then to create a new vision for yourself. Though afraid or unsure, if you continue to trust your money message and take actions in alignment with this new vision, one day you will find yourself living that new life.

Initially, as you are creating you new money message and experimenting with it, you may feel a bit uncomfortable about it. Your money message may even feel a bit false and too unrealistic. That is to be expected. You've lived all of your life up until this moment weighed down by your money baggage. After all, you have a lot of evidence that your money baggage is true, and you may have no evidence—zero, none, zip—that your new money message is true.

Your money message is like new shoes that take a while to break in. Your money baggage, however, is like an old pair of comfortable slippers. It is human nature to stay with what is more known and comfortable. These old slippers are your old patterns of thought. And sometimes those old thoughts come back and inhibit us from acting in line with our money message.

It happened to me recently concerning a decision I faced. I needed to expand my business, to add more office space and hire more employees. As I turned the details over in my mind, I became increasingly anxious. I was wondering about a downturn in the economy. I was worried about the added overhead, and that we wouldn't have the business to support it. I knew I would have to work harder to support the growth. So there I was, smack dab in the middle of my old money baggage again: *I have to work really hard to make money, and even if I do, I'll never make enough.*

One morning, I was fretting about all of this when I remembered my money message. *It is my birthright to have abundance in all areas of my life and I give generously from this abundance.* I breathed deeply a few times and began to reorient my thoughts back around my money message.

Even though it was a stretch to expand my business, I went ahead. Over the ensuing months I experienced a few moments of panic, but I decided to trust and keep going. I hired the staff I needed and as a result have been able to serve more clients and become more profitable as a business.

When I give money away, with every check, with every donation, I trust it will come back to me multifold so I don't have to live in the scarcity of holding on. This trust allows me the courage to take new actions, take more steps, and to keep on when I get afraid.

In Charles Dickens's *A Christmas Carol*, after Scrooge has his awakening, he takes some actions right away that mirror his new world view. We might assume that Scrooge's money baggage is: *I need more, more, more. Money is more important than love.* When his night messengers come and take him on his series of dreams, he is able to witness the sadness and pain his closed heart has caused in the world. Finally, he is taken to see his own grave. When he wakes and finds out he is still alive, Scrooge undergoes a complete change in consciousness. We might say he has discovered his new money message: *Living my life from a place of generosity will make me richer than I could ever imagine.*

He doesn't just think this; he immediately sets out and takes action. He tells the boy in the street to go and buy the biggest turkey he can find and have it delivered to Bob Cratchit's house. He is filled with a joy and newfound generosity in his heart, and he shouts that joy to the world.

If we could follow Scrooge throughout the rest of his life, there would inevitably be times when he would find himself back in his money baggage, alone on a cold night counting his money, wondering how he could get more, and feeling the old fear that propelled his greed. But he would have already taken some baby steps to start to turn his life around. He'd bought a turkey for a poor family. He'd called out good cheer to the people in the streets. Maybe over time, he would have built a new home for the Cratchits or an orphanage for all the street waifs running about.

Changing your reality involves a dance with faith, and requires you to act. You don't take your new money message up to a mountaintop and sit in its glory, expecting your life to be transformed, wanting the universe to do it all. Nor will just verbalizing your money message over and over make a difference.

There is an old Zen saying, "Before enlightenment, chop wood, carry water. After enlightenment, chop wood, carry water." Even after turning over a new leaf, even after insights, the work is still there to do, the action still there to implement.

If you are going to have a new life empowered by your money message, you need to decide what actions are consistent with the money message, and then get out and take them. If you do, good things are going to happen to you. This practice will become a habit, and after some time you will find yourself living amidst a new reality and relationship to money.

CHAPTER 16

MONEY MESSAGE PRINCIPLE #4:
WE CAN ONLY THINK ONE THOUGHT AT A TIME

*S*everal years back I was in Hawaii after a conference with the afternoon to myself and decided to lounge around and read. I chose a spot on a cliff overlooking the ocean with palm trees surrounding me. I read until the sun went down and I couldn't see the words anymore. I sat for some time looking at the sunset, and a canopy of stars began to appear. I was suddenly overwhelmed by a feeling of my puniness in relation to the universe. Here I was, leading a workshop to help people transform their relationship to money and connect with a larger, deeper meaning to their lives, and I felt like a speck of dust in the grand scheme of the cosmos. Who did I think I was anyway? Surrounded by this immense beauty and peace, I wallowed in thoughts of my insignificance.

Somewhere amidst my wallowing I realized I had dropped back into my money baggage mentality, so I counteracted it by remembering my money message. As I went back and forth between both of them, I realized it was impossible for me to think about my money baggage and my money message simultaneously. I had to choose one or the other. So which would it be? Would I choose a money baggage thought or a money message thought? What kind of music did I want to hear, the dirge of my money baggage or the peaceful sonata of my money message?

It's been said that it is functionally impossible to hold two thoughts in your conscious mind at the same time. To demonstrate, try this. Close your eyes and imagine the face of your best friend . . . Then imagine a paper clip . . . Switch back and forth between the two images . . . Now try to think of them both at the same time. You can't do it. You can almost do it, but what is really happening, almost imperceptibly, is that there is a switching going on in the microsecond between the two thoughts. You can only think one thought at a time. This is particularly true when you are trying to hold something more complex than a single image in your mind. With a statement as emotionally charged as your money baggage or as visionary as your new money message, you have to choose. Your mind has to settle on one or the other.

It is truly about choice. Are you thinking your money baggage or your money message? It's your call. Our tendency, which we will be susceptible to for the rest of our lives, is to fall back into the money baggage thoughts habitually. But the work is about awareness—becoming more aware of our thoughts and picking the ones that serve our soul, not the ones that support our habits and fears.

This is where the transformation of your life takes a leap forward—by choosing a money message thought instead of a money baggage thought. By doing this as often as you can, moment by moment, over and over, your life will begin to change.

If you find yourself sitting at your desk frustrated and upset because you hate your job, realize you are immersed in your money baggage. At that moment, think about your money message instead, and then take some action aligned with manifesting the kind of job that would nurture your soul.

If you are an artist bemoaning the fact that you do not have money, unearth your money baggage and see if your thoughts are arising from a conditioned belief. Choose instead your money message and see if it doesn't suggest to you a more expansive way to be an artist in the world supporting yourself.

You can make a choice in the moment between your money baggage and your money message. If, for example, you avoid paying your bills, it's likely that your money baggage is at work. So consciously replace your money baggage with your new money message and realize that paying your bills can be an act of self-love. It is taking care of yourself and your responsibilities so you can spend time dreaming of a new future. This is better than worrying and avoiding the bills.

You can only think one thought at a time. To the extent you focus your thoughts on your money *message* instead of your money *baggage*, your life will change and never again be the same.

CHAPTER 17

MONEY MESSAGE PRINCIPLE #5: CHANGE TAKES TIME AND PERSISTENCE

*I*n trying to transform our relationship to and experience with money, the most difficult hurdle we encounter is time. It can take some time to bring about changes in your life. To see the beneficial results from your money message at work, it is going to take persistence and patience. It may take a while for you to break your old habits and guide your mind to begin processing in a new way.

Thoughts are a chemical phenomenon that create neurological pathways in our brains. When we think a thought over and over we reinforce its pathway. By choosing a new thought again and again, like our new money message, we reinforce the pathways that will lead to different thinking patterns.

This work is not about getting rid of the old pathways; in fact, some researchers believe that we can't eliminate our "hard wiring," the thoughts and beliefs about ourselves that we developed during our formative years. The old neurological pathways and reactions will always be there. We can however, create new pathways by focusing on our money message and taking actions consistent with it. The more we do this, the stronger these new neurological pathways become. Eventually our old money baggage pathways begin to wither. We can consciously decide to empower and give our attention to something new in place of the habitual past.

The process of actually transforming your life can take time. When trying to remake your life around a new thought, backsliding is possible. Decades of thoughts and habits influence our behavior. Our old neurological pathways run deep.

But over time and with persistence, the neurological pathways formed by our new money message will run even deeper and lead us to a new empowered life.

We have all experienced trying to change our old behavior, only to have it creep back in over days or weeks. Behavioral changes don't hold for long unless we alter the underlying or sponsoring thought that created the behavior in the first place, in this case replacing our money baggage with our new money message.

If we continue to take consistent action in line with our new money message, our behavior changes and new possibilities appear.

Your life is not going to magically transform right away as you go through this process. You did a lot of work over many years imbedding behaviors and creating perceptions from your money baggage. Your new money message requires the same conviction and effort, but now with conscious intent.

Jacqueline, an interior designer, had money baggage that arose from her family's belief in being honest poor folks, and from their feeling that money was bad. It was better to be poor and honest, they told her, than to have money and be tarnished by unspiritual thoughts. This is how she describes the difference in living a life that was consistent with her money message instead of with her money baggage:

—

I came to a point in my life where all that old money baggage language needed to change. I realized that work and money are not bad. I am working to remove all the emotional charge from those old ideas. Something is emerging from the shadows, and it's me. And I really like it.

—

This is the attitude we need to have to do this work. It is about the slow process of emerging and liking what we see. Little by little, we get there.

Our conscious mind is like a small rowboat on the surface of the great unconscious. We can row, row, row around but mostly we are subject to the currents and whims of the great force beneath us. In doing our soul's work in relation to money, we must dive into the depths of our unconscious. We must also transform the size of our boat. Through consistent thinking and acting with our money message, we create a large and powerful ocean liner that can take us anywhere on the great sea we want to go.

Courage, patience, and persistence are required on this path. As we continue to deconstruct the habits of our old thoughts and consciously reinforce new ones, good things ultimately will come. We develop less and less resistance to the new thoughts and we begin to attract new situations, new ways of looking at the world, and new opportunities.

It will take some time and you might hit some bumps along the way. Forgive yourself and move on. Your new money message way of life will gradually materialize. Baby step after baby step, you will get to a place where your old money baggage way of life is just a memory and a new life of possibilities is open before you.

Let's return to the four main areas of life we covered in Part I, and take a look at how people have brought about this transformation. Their examples show us how some have made profound changes in their relationships, work, finances, and family life by affirming their new money message and taking actions consistent with this new message.

CHAPTER 18

MONEY MESSAGE AND RELATIONSHIPS

*O*ur money baggage often influences our choice in a partner and how we relate to each other as a couple. Oliver and Anita argued about money regularly. It was the central irritant of their marriage and kept them locked in a constant struggle, full of anxiety about money and resentment toward each other. They were trapped in a perpetual conflict because of their respective money baggage. He was concerned with avoiding money and wanted to leave any situation where it was being discussed *(We don't have the money, something is always wrong! I'm out of here!)*. Her money baggage told her that she was bad with money and compelled her to become a compulsive spender *(I'm bad with money and the end is always near)*.

The discovering and exploring of their respective money baggage messages led to a better understanding of each other. A commitment to create new money messages and live lives consistent with those messages saved their marriage.

⟩———⟨

ANITA: This work of discovering our money baggage gave me a profound insight and compassion into how Oliver's traumatic young experiences shaped his particular view of life. And how our relationship and habits were in perfect (albeit discordant) harmony with our thoughts about money. It had an impact on all areas of our marriage.

OLIVER: I was able to transform my relationship with Anita from periodic dislike, contempt, and cynicism to compassion and understanding. I used to say, "This is just how women are!" and "She has no idea what it took for me to make this money, to just waste it on another pair of shoes." Now I am able to ask her genuine questions about money and to allow her to see my vulnerability around it.

ANITA: I discovered that his avoidance and then anger over money was not about me, but about him. It has allowed me to step back and not take things so personally. I have a sense of finally growing up, coming into my own sense of self. I don't have to manipulate, plan, and control things to get what I want. All is well. I am freed up.

—

The couple created new money messages and began to take consistent actions that supported their money messages.

Oliver's money message is: *Money is energy and I am the sun.* Anita's money message has several parts: *I have the life of my dreams, I am the source of miraculous prosperity and abundance. Life is a gift. All is well.*

Since starting their work on money baggage and money messages, they have had only one disagreement about money in the past three years. Oliver now handles the family finances and Anita has become more conscious of her spending habits and has reined them in.

—

ANITA. This work has moved us from conflict to complement.

OLIVER: We have transformed something "unspeakable" into something that brings us closer together.

ANITA: We have a whole new vision of our future together by being able to talk about things and not fight about money.

We used to waste so much time and energy. Now we are involved in new ventures personally and in business. It's all now being built from a strong and supportive partnership.

⌒

Anita and Oliver have continued this work and each discovered their soul's calling to help alleviate the ravages of poverty in the world. They are leaders in an organization whose mission is to develop the political will among nations to deal with poverty. Best of all, they are recreating their relationship and finding new means to commit and to work together. They tell me they have never had so much fun.

Living in accordance with their money messages transformed their relationship from one of fighting and discord around money to a true partnership of support, empowerment, and enjoyment of life and each other.

⌒

OLIVER: My money message reaffirms, and gives me reliable access to knowing and remembering, who I really am—a part of the eternal, a spiritual and inspiring being. Discovering that gave me the ability to see my marriage as this precious sacred entity, one to be cultivated.

⌒

—

CHAPTER 19

MONEY MESSAGE AND WORK

*T*o illustrate the way a new money message can forever change the way you work and the things you focus on, I want to tell you the stories of two people: Mike, who used his new money message to find a more lucrative career and work fewer hours; and Amanda, who learned to keep the money she earned and allow her wealth to support her creativity.

Whatever Mike did, in his father's eyes it was never enough. He could never do enough to earn his dad's love. When he got all A's and two B's, he was told, "You'll have to work a little harder in Social Studies and Spanish." His dad only saw what his son didn't do and only told him what he didn't like.

Mike got a job delivering papers, and later bagging groceries. He became a hard worker. He worked his way all through high school and college.

A few years back Mike came to work for me forty hours a week and then took a second job working twenty hours more during the week and on the weekend. And despite all this hard work, he was also always in debt.

Mike's money baggage is: *I don't make enough money because I never do enough to deserve it.* As a child, Mike got money confused with love. What he truly wanted from his dad was love and recognition. He could never get it, so his young mind decided he wasn't good enough, that he just had to work harder. Without being aware of the reasons why, he threw himself into work to get love and recognition, to fill the void. But he never did fill it. He worked harder and still ended up continuously short of money (love).

He then implemented a new money message in his life: *I earn more money than I will ever need and I share my abundance, love, and joy with all.* He began to take actions to support his new money message. He met with a career counselor and decided to open his own bookkeeping business. He wrote a business plan and discovered that he could support himself as a bookkeeper working a reasonable forty hours a week and not have to work two jobs. He started his bookkeeping business by telling everyone he knew he was looking for clients. In a very short period of time, he had enough clients and he quit working for me.

Today he works less and makes more than he ever has. He sets his own hours and he only works for clients he wants to work for. His life hasn't gone from pizza to caviar, but the struggle is gone and he now feels in charge of his life.

The important lesson from Mike's story is common to every money baggage/money message story: the possibilities are right in front of you—you just can't see them. For Mike, the option for him to open his own business and make more money while working less was there all the time—he just couldn't see it because his money baggage was in the way. It was covering up the real reason he worked so hard and could not get ahead.

He was the same person with the same circumstances the moment after he came up with his new money message as he was before. His new money message simply opened up for him a world of new possibilities. He implemented actions in line with his new money message and then these new opportunities began to shape his life.

Another person whose new money message led to the transformation of her relationship to work was Amanda. Amanda grew up in the Midwest where she attended an exclusive private school with the daughters of multi-millionaires. While her family had a fine life and she doesn't ever remember wanting for things, her friends enjoyed a different life: they lived in big mansions; their budgets for clothes and activities were way beyond Amanda's; and they were dropped off at school by chauffeurs.

She remembers fondly the pool parties and how she loved to spend the night at their mansions. What she remembers less fondly is how her friends' parents treated her. It was as if she wasn't even there, even when she was eating dinner with them. If other girls of multi-millionaires were there, the parents would talk to them, but not to Amanda. She felt that because her family didn't have as much money as they did, she didn't belong at the same table. Her friends' parents seemed to treat her as if she didn't exist.

From these experiences, Amanda decided that rich people were mean and she was determined to never treat anyone as she had been treated. Amanda's money baggage is: *I'm not one of them and I don't want to be one of them.*

Amanda grew up to be a successful divorce attorney. She had plenty of clients and was well respected within the legal community. Her practice continued to grow, as did her revenue. But a funny thing happened—she always found a way to spend her increasing revenue on her business, and her take-home pay stayed the same. She would inevitably find something that needed to be fixed or purchased, or a new business venture that needed to be funded. Somehow, there just wasn't much left over at the end of each month. And if there *was* money left over, she'd give it away to someone who needed it for a class or workshop.

This went on for years, and it frustrated her, but it wasn't until Amanda identified her money baggage that she got a glimmer as to why she didn't bring home more money. She realized that she was finding ways to spend money on her business ventures or give it away so that she "didn't become one of them."

In working on her money baggage, she identified the multitude of ways she managed to get rid of her revenue so that she didn't become like those mean rich people: moving to a bigger office; hiring more staff; not charging as much as other divorce attorneys charge; creating a legal-advice business for the masses, and giving money away to nonprofits.

While Amanda's husband was also working, the low level of her take-home pay didn't affect their day-to-day life that much. But now that he was approaching retirement and she was going to be supporting them, she realized she had to turn the situation around.

She created her new money message: *I freely express my creativity with ease and grace.*

In a period of three short months she raised her rates, terminated an employee who really wasn't getting the job done, and hired a replacement who was immediately able to bill clients for work that more than covered her salary. In addition, she created systems and procedures to streamline the workflow so her firm could take on more clients and generate more revenue; collected old accounts payable that had been long overdue; and started requesting a retainer from clients before she would start working on their divorce, something she'd always been afraid to do. Today her billings are up and she is on the road to taking home more than she ever has. She now knows that if she takes home more money, she won't become "one of them." For she can "freely express her creativity with ease and grace" and support her family, and her soul. As Amanda said to me, "When you say money baggage, you're not kidding. It is such a relief to discover what has been holding me back. I'm excited about moving forward into my wide open future."

Your money baggage will express the underlying attitudes and beliefs that have led you to your current work or your lack of it. Your new money message will guide you to the work and life you imagine yourself doing in the future, full of possibilities just waiting for you to discover and explore. These possibilities are there, right now in your life. It's up to you to dive into the process and discover the new relationship to work that awaits you, one that cares for your soul in matters of money.

CHAPTER 20

MONEY MESSAGE AND FINANCE

The stories in this book all illustrate that if you alter your relationship to money, your life and world will be a different place. This is especially true in the arena of personal finance. If we investigate the issues we have about money, implement a new money message, and take actions aligned with it, money will no longer be a source of suffering. I quote here Judy's story at length, because of how well it illustrates, step by step, how she followed these concepts and how it affected her relationship to her personal finances.

At the time I took the Caring for Your Soul in Matters of Money® workshop, life had not been kind. Since the finalization of my divorce a year before, I had been struggling

139

financially. I had not received the divorce payout that was due from my ex-husband and had no savings. I was juggling every month to make ends meet with two daughters at home and one in college.

It was obvious to me that I was a worrier, but what I discovered in the workshop was that not everyone operated with the same constant, nagging mental chatter that I did.

I also discovered my money baggage: *I have to work hard, I'm not supposed to want anything, and I don't deserve anything anyway.*

Standing in the shower in the mornings or while driving back and forth to work, I would always do mental arithmetic. I'd be trying to figure out how much the bills were, how to pay them, and still have money for groceries or any unexpected things that might come up.

I rarely balanced my checkbook, so I really didn't know how much I had available for paying the bills. I usually didn't pay bills by the due date because I never wanted to let go of the money. I might write the checks and seal the envelopes, but not mail them for a few days. The whole schizoid attitude was instrumental in feeding my worrier nature.

At the workshop, I created my new money message: *I have plenty to live freely and give freely.*

I decided to really discipline myself to think my money message and take actions consistent with it instead of with my money baggage. I posted my money message on the bathroom mirror, in my checkbook, and in the middle of my car's steering wheel.

I worked out a money plan for the next twelve months so I could see what my expenses and income were. The money plan clearly showed that I didn't have enough income to cover my monthly expenses. Yikes!

Yet instead of going into my worrier tailspin, I decided to get a second job to help cover all the expenses and get out of the hole I was in. Almost immediately I was offered a job that I could do on the weekends and get paid a substantial amount per hour. I worked that job for a year until I had the income I needed to pay all my expenses every month.

I set up an accounting program on my computer and got a new bank account so I could download all the bank transactions directly into the accounting program. I categorized all the expenses so I could see where my money was really going and if I was on target with the money plan I set up for myself. As I tracked all my expenses, I went back to the plan and modified it as I began to get a clearer picture of how much I actually spent each month and on what.

I also set up as many of the bills as possible to direct debit out of my checking account, so I didn't have to be bothered with writing checks and mailing them. Since I had a steady job and got a paycheck twice a month, all I had to do was get my paycheck deposited in a timely manner. I contacted my creditors and asked to change some of the due dates on my bills to make my cash flow work better. I made some substantial payments on my three credit cards every month until I paid them off.

I worked with the Child Support Services and began to receive the monthly child support that was due, instead of listening to my money baggage, which says, *"I am not supposed to want anything, and I don't deserve anything anyway."*

One of my daughters wanted to go back to playing cello in the school orchestra and I told her she could because music is one of her passions. At the time, I didn't have any way to pay for the rental of the cello, but I was listening to my money message, *I have plenty to live freely and give freely* and knew we would come up with a way to make it work. As we were enrolling her in the orchestra class at school, the music teacher said she had a cello she could use. She walked us back to the music classroom, went to the storage closet, and took out the cello. My daughter was thrilled.

Another daughter had been attending the same private school for years. As I came to see the reality of my financial situation, I told the school's director that she would not be able to attend the following year because it was no longer affordable for me. The director said that my daughter's presence in the school made a contribution to the school and she insisted she attend. The director told me I should pay whatever I could afford. I paid about a quarter of the normal tuition for the next two years until she graduated.

I worked with my daughter in college to get financial aid so she could complete the last two years of college, which she was able to do.

I began contributing to my favorite charitable organization every month.

When the kids asked for things, I could say yes or no based on knowing where I stood financially. This is a much calmer, saner, more peaceful way to operate instead of the old way where I would say yes to almost everything and then fret about how to make the money work.

Each month on the spreadsheet showing the monthly expenses and income, I also kept a list of items that did not fit into the budget; this became our wish list. The items on it were both large and small—vacation, driving school tuition, a car for my youngest daughter, a guitar, camera, etc. Interestingly, many of these things began to show up.

For example, a co-worker said she was going to sell the car of her recently deceased mother. It was the perfect first vehicle for my youngest daughter. I bought it from my co-worker at a bargain price and she was excited that it was going to someone who would really appreciate it.

Although having all the material things "show up" has been good, what have been the best results are the other less tangible ones like:

- *Having peace of mind*, not the old fretting, worrying, anxiety, and mental gymnastics.
- *Being responsible*, not avoiding things, just standing firmly in my money message and making choices.
- *Feeling confident*, experiencing success and using the evidence of my successes as my stepping stones for whatever is next.
- *Using creativity and inventiveness*, finding the means to do and have things beyond what I had done before. This often means asking others for help—something I would never do when operating from my money baggage, as I always had to work hard and not want anything.

- *Being excited about life*, enjoying every day, and laughing a lot.
- *Having a vision for the future*, allowing myself desires, dreams, and possibilities.

∽

One step at a time, we get closer to a future that becomes our present, where we feel more alert, alive, and aware in our lives. Each step builds on the one before it. Judy's money situation did not change instantly after she started this work. She just kept putting one foot consciously in front of the other, firmly planting it in her money message. Eventually those steps bore fruit and gave her a sense of direction and control over her personal finances that she had never before thought possible.

CHAPTER 21

MONEY MESSAGE AND FAMILY

$\mathcal{C}$reating a new money message can have a profound impact on the health of a family. Here are two stories, both about men who changed the entire dynamic of their respective home lives by taking actions—big steps in one case, small steps in the other—consistent with their new money message.

Remember Wendell, the CPA whose dad had a car dealership and worked so hard he never had time to spend with Wendell? Wendell concluded deep inside that money is more important than family. As an adult he modeled his work life after his dad and missed out on ten years of his own kids' lives.

Here is Wendell's new money message: *I live a life balanced in stewardship, praying to God with a grateful heart, nurturing my family, sharing my giftedness with others, and giving back from the first fruits of my labor.*

—

I've become the dad I didn't have. I left the big accounting firm and started my own business, so I can spend more time with my family. I now have my own successful CPA practice providing accounting, financial planning, and investment advice to families and small businesses.

I spend time with my kids every day. I make them breakfast and I help take them to drum lessons, doctor's appointments, baseball practice, and Cub Scouts. When they are sick, I stay home with them. I rarely work beyond 5 p.m., I volunteer at both their schools, and once a month the entire family picks a great place to go out to dinner together. I had never done any of these kinds of things before.

In a funny kind of way, my money message isn't about money. Instead, taking action in line with my new money message has allowed me to have deep and satisfying relationships with my children. I have talks with them that I never imagined I'd ever have. I won't pass up spending quality times with my kids for anything—especially work.

—

Then there's Phillip, who had always felt secure as a child, but who came home from school one day to learn from his mother that they were having financial problems. Phillip said it was as if a trap door had opened in the floor and suddenly he was free falling into an abyss of uncertainty. He no longer felt safe.

This experience, and a series of choices to counteract that feeling of insecurity, shaped his life. He grew up to be a successful and wealthy doctor. As long as Phillip had lots of money he felt safe.

Phillip married an incredibly bright, entrepreneurial woman whom he adored. They were partners in all areas of their relationship, except for money, where they had very different styles. While she loved giving presents at holidays, he felt it was a complete waste of time and money. He could never figure out what gift to give, and his mood always put a damper on the festivities.

Spending in general was a sore spot. When his wife would wear a new outfit he would say, "Is that new? How much did it cost? Did you really need it?" Never did he say, "Gee, honey, that outfit looks great on you." His wife felt guilty buying anything, and when she did, his attitude took much of the fun out of it.

And he had this habit of squishing the tail end of an old bar of soap on top of the new bar, which drove his wife nuts. Here was a doctor, making plenty of money, squishing soap bars together.

In addition to driving his wife nuts, he also never felt relaxed; he always worried. Phillip's money baggage is: *I have to be frugal and work long and hard to make money and there is never more than enough and if I don't have enough, I'm not safe.*

In discovering his money baggage, Phillip saw how all of his actions and choices affected his wife and kids. Holidays had a certain tone and his family all recognized that certain stressed look on his face. His money baggage was sucking the fun out of the family festivities. All because he thought he needed money to feel safe.

Phillip was determined to turn this around. He created his new money message: *I'm grateful for the ever-increasing extraordinary abundance of creativity, health, wealth, leisure, pleasure, service, and contribution that flows through me now and always with ease. I am safe, whole, fulfilled, and capable with my abundant wealth. It is so fun and easy. Thank you, God.*

The actions Phillip decided to take with his money message in mind weren't big or earth-shattering. He simply started telling his wife how beautiful she was when she wore a new outfit—without giving her the third degree about whether she needed it or not. He took his wife out shopping for her birthday and didn't complain about how much her new outfit cost. He told his wife he wanted to be responsible for buying their two daughters presents for Christmas. He stopped squishing soap bars together.

To most people, these actions might seem small and insignificant, but to Phillip's wife and children they completely changed the mood in the home. Phillip felt more relaxed. No one had to walk around on eggshells, worrying about what Dad was thinking. The mood, especially around holidays, was one of fun and play.

Phillip so clearly illustrates that when it comes to family, the slightest changes can make a major difference. Today, he says, "I say my money message all the time. It feels good. It feels real—it really does." At one point, he added the word "contribution" to his money message, after having a new insight: "My frugality, that came out of my need to be safe, wouldn't let me be generous. Contribution opens up the flow so that I can do all the things I wanted to do but couldn't, because I was so frugal. That's all changed."

Discovering your new money message and taking actions in the world compatible with it is a transforming experience. It is going to take a bit of tenacity and constant focus on your new money message to pull it off. But the work is worth it. Imagine what it will be like for you to have a more conscious and collaborative relationship with money. Watch how that also changes the relationships to those closest to you. Go ahead, create your money message and then take actions consistent with it. Your family deserves it and so do you.

CHAPTER 22

⌣

CONTINUING THE JOURNEY:
EXERCISES FOR KEEPING YOUR MONEY MESSAGE ALIVE

*L*ife does not often proceed in a straight line. On our journey to transform our relationship with money, we should not expect things to move in a strictly linear fashion. This is the nature of the work in making the subconscious conscious: it moves in a spiraling and expanding manner as it transforms us. Other times it is halting, two steps forward and one step back. But these baby steps are always taking you higher and, paradoxically, further inward in a spiral of learning and experiencing. As your awareness grows and you develop more inward harmony, so too will the details of your outer life tend toward harmony.

When we decide to explore our pain, denial, and confusion about money, we consciously engage in the Hero's journey to find out who we are and why we are here. This nonlinear journey involves never-ending discovery and adventure.

The work of transforming our relationship to money will not happen accidentally. It won't happen on its own. And it won't happen unless you keep with it. It takes determination to keep your new money message alive. Your money baggage has influenced your life for many years up to this point. It will never go away completely.

Stand firmly in the strength of your money message. The tendency for your resolve to weaken is only natural. Given that you can only think one thought at a time, eventually your money message thoughts will take over and replace your money baggage thinking if you remain conscious and determined.

Here are some simple exercises, ways for you to keep your money message vibrant and evolving in your life.

- *Post your money message where you will see it often:*

On your refrigerator	Next to the telephone
Next to the light switch	On your computer monitor
On your dashboard	In your wallet or checkbook
On your bathroom mirror	

- *Use an alert tone on your PDA or email program* to remind you daily of your new money message.

- *Set up a weekly call with a pal* to share stories of successes and failures in implementing your new money message.
- *Create a list and add evidence* that your new money message is working.
- *Keep evolving your new money message.* Periodically revisit it and see if you want to update it or revise it.
- *Make collages of your money baggage and your money message.* Collages tap into your powers of visualization, an extremely effective way to create the life you desire.

Making the collages can be an especially rewarding process. Begin with your money baggage collage, and follow these steps:

- *Get a large piece of paper or poster board, at least 8.5x11.* Write or type your money baggage statement at the top.
- *Get a bunch of magazines.* You don't have to have any specific type of magazine, just get a variety. Some good magazines to use include *National Geographic*; *Newsweek*; money and finance magazines; and architectural, travel, and cooking magazines.
- *Look through the magazines,* cutting out images or pictures that communicate to you the essence of your money baggage. Find plenty of images; you should have more than enough to cover your entire sheet.

- *Arrange the images on the sheet.* In arranging, let the images speak to you. You will know where to put them once you start playing with their placement.
- *Paste the images onto the sheet,* letting the edges overlap to fill every bit of blank space.

Follow the same process for your money message collage, this time using pictures or images that communicate to you the essence of your new money message.

Have fun with this creative process. When an image speaks to you, cut it out. Don't filter; don't let your inner critic voice keep you from using an image. There are no right or wrong images. Your subconscious will speak to you; you just need to be willing to listen.

You can use words but only sparingly. Primarily you want to use images or pictures. You want someone to be able to look at your collages and get an idea of what your money baggage or money message is just by looking at it.

When you have completed both collages, stand back and look at the visual difference between the two. Note what emotions and thoughts arise when you look at your money baggage collage versus your money message collage. Discuss these observations with your friends and family, or write them down to review later.

Put your money message collage up where you will see it often and where it will serve as a strong visual reminder of your new money message. Use it to help inspire you and shape your life. The constant reminder of your vision and dreams, of where you are headed, will help reinforce your intention to keep your actions consistent with your money message, and remind you to keep listening to your soul.

When you are done comparing the two collages, you may want to put your money baggage collage away, but in a place, perhaps a file drawer, where you can refer back to it later.

Here are a couple of examples of what people's collages looked like after doing this exercise:

JUDY'S MONEY BAGGAGE: *I have to work hard, I'm not supposed to want anything, and I don't deserve anything anyway.*

JUDY'S MONEY BAGGAGE COLLAGE: The images are almost all in black-and-white. There's a woman at the top of an old decrepit ladder looking very scared; a heart with a piece of barbed wire going through it; masses of people in front of a dollar sign; a woman exhausted with her head on her desk.

JUDY'S MONEY MESSAGE: *I have plenty, to live freely, and give freely.*

JUDY'S MONEY MESSAGE COLLAGE: I have a woman with a smile on her face with up-stretched arms that communicate "I love my life"; flowers; $1000 dollar bills; a family obviously in love; images of nature and the beach.

⎯

SHERRY'S MONEY BAGGAGE: *I'm no good with money.*

SHERRY'S MONEY BAGGAGE COLLAGE: Broken dishes; someone "pulling her hair out" while slumped over a checkbook; a thundercloud with a tornado; a stack of bills.

SHERRY'S MONEY MESSAGE: *I am an expert steward of all the abundance the universe provides me and I give back to the world in plentiful and creative ways.*

SHERRY'S MONEY MESSAGE COLLAGE: Image of earth from space; a meadow filled with flowers surrounded by a forest; hands palm up in front of a person as if they have just given something to someone else; someone painting a picture.

⎯

You will find that the contrast between your two collages is sharp and distinct. The money baggage collage can be almost painful to look at. The money message collage conjures up a sense of peace, power, fun, and possibility. You may find you want to look at it and dream for a long time.

I have done workshops where people who have never done a collage in their life get totally immersed in the process. They surprise themselves and their spouses or partners by how creatively and perfectly the collages communicate their money baggage and their money message.

Allow yourself to be creative. Figure out what will work for you. Do something fun every day that will remind you of your money message. Keep it alive, keep it alive, keep it alive . . .

CHAPTER 23

TRANSLATION: A POWERFUL TOOL

*W*hen we create a new money message, we begin to see new possibilities in our lives. It's as if we are wearing a special lens, the lens of our money message, through which we can finally see more color, more resources, more options. Our old lens, the lens of our money baggage, limits our perception—like looking at a bowl of M&Ms® and seeing only the brown and yellow ones. With the money message lens, suddenly we see all the colors that had been impossible to see before, though they were there all along.

Once you create a money message and begin to take actions aligned with it, a peaceful, calm, self-trusting person begins to develop, and frustration and doubt recede. You begin to see new possibilities, options you couldn't see or even imagine before. You start making decisions using your new money message to clarify your direction and guide your life.

All of us will eventually bump up against something that will bring our money baggage right back in front of us; we will forget our money message, not to mention the possibilities it allows. Maybe you find a new job where it seems as if life is flowing, but then find a few months later that you still are having trouble managing your spending habits. Or maybe you find that the number of hours you are working is creeping up to an unreasonable level. No matter what the circumstances, without knowing it, you'll begin to operate from your money baggage again. It happens automatically, unconsciously. At this point many people get frustrated, feel hopeless, and give up.

To get you through these bumpy places, I designed a powerful tool I call a translation. A *translation* is an exercise in which you first look at an issue through the lens of your old money baggage, and then you consider the same issue through the lens of your new money message. It's a deceptively simple but effective way to allow your money message to express itself in specific areas of your life.

Let me give you an example of a translation I did recently. An employee came in one day and gave her two-week notice. It was a particularly busy time at work and I already had several projects I was working on. When she gave her notice I thought to myself, *This is the last thing I want to deal with. I don't have time. I'll never get someone hired before she goes and then she won't be around to train them.* After I took a breath, I realized that my money baggage was screaming at me, telling me that I had to work hard and it wasn't going to turn out.

At that moment I did a translation. I wrote my money baggage down on the top of a sheet of paper: *You have to work hard to make money, and even if you do, you'll never make enough.* Under it I wrote what my thoughts would be regarding hiring a new employee looking through the lens of my money baggage. They were: *Finding a new employee will be hard. I'll never find one by the time my current employee leaves. I don't have time to write the advertisement for the paper and interview a bunch of people who won't work out anyway.* I was in a downward spiral, not seeing any possibilities for solving the problem in time.

On the other side of the paper I wrote my money message: *It is my birthright to effortlessly have abundance in all areas of my life and I give generously from this abundance.* Underneath that I wrote what my thoughts would be regarding hiring a new employee if I looked through the lens of my new money message. They were: *I will effortlessly find the perfect employee, who will be trained by my current employee before she leaves.*

At that instant I saw the appropriate actions to take consistent with my new money message. I called my current employee and told her to write an advertisement to be posted on a job placement bulletin board at a local university which offers financial planning courses. I booked out six hours on my calendar to interview candidates and waited. In less than a week several qualified people submitted their resumés.

We had six candidates come in for interviews and four of them were equally qualified and perfect for the job. The hardest part was picking which to hire from the four best candidates. The first candidate I offered the job to accepted and was at work two hours later. For the next two days he trained with the employee that was leaving.

Having my thoughts be shaped by my money message rather than my money baggage instantly opened me back up to the possibilities for how to handle the situation, options that were there all along, but which I couldn't see as long as my money baggage was influencing me. Once I focused on my money message, new avenues of action became obvious.

Translations are very simple and effective. If you do them whenever you feel stuck about something, new possibilities will quickly become apparent to you.

To do a translation, turn to WORKSHEET 5: TRANSLATION in the Appendix, or take a blank piece of paper and divide it into two columns. Write your money baggage at the top of the left column, and your new money message at the top of the right column.

Then pick the area to do a translation on—say, paying the bills. Write in the left column under your money baggage how your money baggage is shaping your thoughts and behavior around paying bills. Looking through your money baggage lens, you may say: *I dread even looking at the bills because I'll always just be squeaking by.*

Then move to the right side of the page and write down the thought about paying bills as seen from your new money message perspective. Looking through your money message lens, you might say: *I am completely accountable and use inventiveness and all the resources and magic of the universe to have what I want.*

With this new perspective, seen through your money message lens, you might schedule a time twice a month to pay your bills. You might even ask a friend to join you and bring their bills along so you can have fun and find mutual support, turning a once-dreaded chore into a pleasant task. Or if you are married, you could ask your partner if he or she would be willing to take over the bill-paying responsibilities in exchange for you doing something that he doesn't particularly enjoy doing but you wouldn't mind doing at all. You could set up as many of your bills to be paid automatically as possible. You could hire a bookkeeper to pay your bills.

The possibilities for solving any problem are there before you all the time; you just can't see them as options because of the narrow view through your money baggage lens.

Doing translations allows you to realign yourself with how you really want your life to be in specific areas. A translation can help not only with the small details of life but the large details as well. Anita and Oliver do translations regularly. Here's a dramatic example of how a translation exercise helped them sell their farm.

Looking through their money baggage lenses about selling the farm they wrote: *Financial disaster is looming if the farm doesn't sell.*

They wanted to sell the farm but subdivide the property so they could keep the house they had been living in. They listed the farm and for two years had no offers. Their financial assets began to dwindle.

They decided to do a translation on selling the farm. From their money message lenses they came up with: *We will find the perfect buyer and the perfect price, the perfect completion and the perfect relationship with the new owner.*

—

OLIVER: It was unbelievable! The day after this translation we got an offer and received six more offers in the next two months.

ANITA: One of the offers was a very honest and quiet man who told us he wanted to operate the farm and respect it as if it was still ours.

OLIVER: He gave us just the price we wanted. And miraculously, the provincial and municipal governments made three favorable rulings critical to the closing and the deal was done.

ANITA: We, along with our realtor, were truly shocked at the speed at which it happened. And what's more, the new buyer not only wanted us to stay in the house but he wanted to landscape our yard as a show property for his nursery business.

—

Along with doing translations whenever they feel moved to, Oliver and Anita keep their respective money messages strong in their lives on a daily basis. Oliver carries his money message in his wallet and also puts it up on his bathroom mirror.

—

When I am upset and can't see any options regarding a situation I say to myself my money message: *Money is energy and I am the sun.* Immediately I stop being afraid. I ask myself, "Is the sun scared?"

My money message reminds me who I really am; how blessed I am with my health, my family, my friends; and that I have everything it takes to do what I set my mind to. It literally and immediately alters the state I am in, as I allow myself to be the capable, creative person I know I am.

—

Once you have your new money message well in hand, and you make efforts to keep it in front of you, and begin to take baby steps and actions consistent with it, watch for those areas of life where you bump up against obstacles. Then sit down and do a translation on that area. Figure out specific actions you can take to move in accord with this new translation.

You can do a translation on any area of your life: money, health, relationships, taking care of yourself, charging what you are worth, or finding a new home.

Translations are transformational. Given that you can only think one thought at a time, a translation reminds you to be conscious of which thoughts you are thinking, which thoughts are shaping your life. A translation triggers you to reorient your unconscious thoughts and to consciously choose which thoughts you want to base your actions on.

As we near the end of this book and you start on your journey, let me review the seven basic steps in transforming your relationship to money:

1. Discover and write your money baggage.
2. Become aware of how your money baggage has shaped your life.
3. Create a new money message.
4. Take actions consistent with your new money message.
5. Use translations in any area of your life that isn't going as smoothly as you would like.
6. Continue to take actions consistent with your new money message.
7. Build on the results. Notice and collect evidence about how your new money message is influencing your life and keep at it.

And get ready for your life to change. Every time you take actions consistent with your money message, you are creating new neurological pathways to influence your life going forward—pathways that care for your soul.

CHAPTER 24

~

CARING FOR YOUR SOUL IN MATTERS OF MONEY

*O*ur lives are sacred. And since money affects everything in our lives, this work of discovering our money baggage and activating our new money message is sacred work. It comes from our soul. That is why the language of our new money message is so clear and simple.

When we listen to what our soul is saying through our new money message, it will lead us to the reason we are here, to our true work and purpose in life—as Jacob Needleman says, to "become what we are meant to be."

Each of us has a unique gift to share with our community or world. A gift the world is longing for. This gift, when it is a true expression of the soul, inspires others, is a joy to give, and brings a sense of purpose and meaning to our life. I believe we each have a higher purpose, and that money is an access point by which we can discover or express our gift. When we give that gift to the world, we are caring for our soul.

Maybe your gift is being a great and noble friend. Maybe your gift is to be the artist you've always longed to be. Perhaps your purpose is to assist nonprofits in raising more money, or to teach kids how to sail.

Your gift might be to develop powerful new software that helps insurance companies better serve their customers. Maybe you are a great soccer coach and your gift is to inspire and teach kids teamwork. Maybe you see cooking as a high art and want to follow that, or you need to travel the planet and write about your adventures. Perhaps your gift is to be the best mom or dad or grandma or grandpa or sister or brother you can be. Or maybe you simply need to love and accept yourself and become truly who you are—this might be your gift to the world. Others might be helped and inspired by your wisdom and energy.

Don't feel that you have to invent the next miracle drug to heal some disease or save the planet (though many people who implement a new money message do actually find meaningful work helping others). The point of all of this is to find more peace of mind around money and why you are here. Your new money message will guide you. It is a voice that can be trusted. It is coming from the same place everyone's new money message comes from—the deep well of your soul. Listen.

If only everyone did what he or she really loved to do, what an incredible place this world would be. What if the people who really love to drive buses were bus drivers? You'd know it the moment you got on the bus. If everyone followed their heart—tried out for a play or started a nonprofit to help homeless women, or became an organic farmer, or a wooden boat builder—we'd be happier. We would do more good in the world because we would be more content; people would be inspired just by being around us.

What if we let our souls speak through us and then took actions to follow that voice? Our lives would be more purposeful and more helpful to others.

George Bernard Shaw wrote, in a letter dedicating his play *Man and Superman*, "This is the true joy in life, the being used for a purpose recognized by yourself as a mighty one." Also attributed to him are the words "I am of the opinion that my life belongs to the whole community, and as long as I live, it is my privilege to do for it whatever I can."

When we create our new money message, we create pathways that are honest and authentic expressions of who we truly are. We will find that this truer self, this more expansive, more peaceful, more effective self has always been there, but it was masked inside our money baggage, suppressing our essence. The purpose of our money message is to give ourselves a new way to look at the world so we can fully express who we are in all areas of our lives.

As I have lived a life consistent with my money message, I've noticed how I look at life differently, and how my actions line up with this new way of looking. And I've found my soul's calling—helping people heal their issues about money and give their unique gift to the world. It is my vision to have money be a source of freedom, power, and full self-expression for every person on the planet.

I start with my family: I am conscious every day of what message about money I give to my children. I want them to see it as an empowering force in their lives, in every way. I personally strive to live each day in balance—personally, professionally, and spiritually. For I know, deep down, in the depths of my heart, that we can all be at peace with money. We no longer have to suffer over it.

It can be a source of freedom and power in our lives. We can express who and what we were truly meant to be and money doesn't have to stop us any longer. It is about creating a new life. Your new money message will naturally connect to all levels of your life, the physical, emotional, mental, and spiritual, because it is being directed from your soul.

We can build a vital new life around our money message. Our thoughts create our reality, as the words of Buddha Shakyamuni express: "We are what we think. All that we are arises with our thoughts. With our thoughts we make the world." So, the practice is to ensure that our thoughts are in line with our highest dreams for our life and our contribution to the world.

Our money baggage comes from a place where our heart has been hurt. We don't realize that at first; we might resist the idea. I know many people who shrug off this idea that they are hurt, but every person I have seen go through the process of discovering their money baggage and who contemplates it deeply finds pain that is asking to be healed.

When our heart is hurt there are only certain ways we can respond to the universe. And the universe will respond to us in kind. If we feel limited or of low self-worth or if we feel driven to achieve because we don't feel loved, the universe will allow us to manifest only the conditions that support that belief.

We can heal our hearts. We can create a new money message and activate it. With healed hearts we can really make a difference in our lives and in the world.

Which inner voice will you listen to? Your old money baggage or your new money message? One of them is active within you right now. A thought has been behind the formation of every moment of your life. Your money baggage or new money message is forming your present reality right now. You can only think one thought at a time. You have a choice. Which will it be?

Look to your thoughts and let your new money message guide your actions. What are you passionate about? What difference might you make in your life and in the world? What is your soul calling you to do?

~

YOUR PERSONAL HISTORY IN MATTERS OF MONEY

*H*ow does your relationship with money affect your life? Your feelings about money have evolved from what you have observed, heard, experienced, and ultimately decided in your past. This money baggage is a heavy burden you have carried everywhere. Use the following worksheets to explore questions that will help uncover your personal history in matters of money. Notice that what different parts of you say about money may be contradictory. That's okay; just keep writing whatever comes to mind.

WORKSHEET 1: MONEY IN MY YOUNGER YEARS

Use your own memories to answer these questions. You can also interview family members, or go through old photos for anything that will help you remember how the subject of money was handled in your childhood.

1. *How did you relate to money as a child? Did you feel "poor" or "rich" or somewhere in between?*

_____

_____

_____

2. *What are your earliest memories of money?*

_____

_____

_____

3. *What is your happiest memory with money? Your unhappiest?*

_____

_____

_____

4. What did your parents say about money—nothing, or a lot? How about your other family members?

_____

_____

_____

_____

5. How did your parents' opinions about money differ?

_____

_____

_____

_____

6. How did your family communicate about money? What was said or not said to you about money?

_____

_____

_____

_____

WORKSHEET 2: MONEY IN MY ADULT YEARS

Examine the way you relate to money now. Look at your feelings, habits, and the things you say about money. Be as nonjudgmental and honest as possible.

1. *What are your fears about money?*

   _____

   _____

   _____

   _____

2. *What are your worries about your future? Are you anxious about money?*

   _____

   _____

   _____

   _____

3. *Are you generous or stingy?*

   _____

   _____

   _____

   _____

4. *Do you treat? Do you tip?*

_____

_____

_____

_____

5. *What do your friends say about money?*

_____

_____

_____

_____

6. *If you have a spouse/partner, what does he or she say about money?*

_____

_____

_____

_____

7. *What do you say about money?*

_____

_____

_____

_____

WORKSHEET 3: DISCOVERING MY MONEY BAGGAGE

Your money baggage—an erroneous decision you made about money as a child—made its way into your subconscious and affected your life in unique ways. To discover your money baggage and the ways it operates in your life now, carefully look at all the information from Worksheets 1 and 2, and then distill them into one statement that captures the essence of your limiting relationship to money. Then write down how your money baggage has influenced each area of your life listed on the next page.

EXAMPLE:

MY MONEY BAGGAGE IS: *Rich people are mean.*

RELATIONSHIPS: If I make more money than I need to get by, I'll lose all of my friends.

CAREER: I can't have a job where I make a lot of money.

My Money Baggage Is: _____

_____

_____

It influences these areas of my life in the following ways:

Relationships:_____

_____

Career:_____

_____

Finances: _____

_____

Family: _____

_____

Health: _____

_____

Home: _____

_____

Paying bills:_____

_____

Buying gifts: _____

_____

Hobbies: _____

_____

WORKSHEET 4: CREATING MY MONEY MESSAGE

Listening to your soul, you will find clues about how a new relationship with money can put you in alignment with your purpose in life. Take time to dream, to listen quietly, to imagine. Ask your soul what are its highest thoughts about money? What is it telling you to do? What is your purpose here? How can you fully express what you want to do with your life? After careful listening, distill the answers you get into one statement—your new money message. Then write down the ways in which a positive, empowering view toward money will influence each different area of your life listed on the next page.

EXAMPLE:

MY MONEY MESSAGE IS: *Money is a valuable tool, and I can use it with skill, humility, and awareness.*

RELATIONSHIPS: My friends and I find creative ways to spend time together while contributing to our community.

CAREER: I am successful in my career. I do more good with my wealth than I could ever do being "virtuous" in just getting by.

MY MONEY MESSAGE IS: _____

_____

_____

It influences these areas of my life in the following ways:

RELATIONSHIPS:_____

_____

CAREER:_____

_____

FINANCES: _____

_____

FAMILY: _____

_____

HEALTH: _____

_____

HOME: _____

_____

PAYING BILLS:_____

_____

BUYING GIFTS: _____

_____

HOBBIES: _____

_____

WORKSHEET 5: TRANSLATION

In doing a translation, you first see an issue through the lens of your old money baggage, and then consider the same issue though the lens of your new money message. Translations are a way to apply your new money message to specific areas of your life. To do that, write your money baggage and your money message at the top of each column. Then take a situation that you want to translate into your new way of thinking and compare how that situation looks through each of your "lenses."

EXAMPLE:

MONEY BAGGAGE: *I have to work hard, I'm not supposed to want anything, and I don't deserve anything anyway.*

MONEY MESSAGE: *I have plenty to live freely and give freely.*

SITUATION: Paying bills

MONEY BAGGAGE SAYS: I dread even looking at the bills because I'll always just be squeaking by.

MONEY MESSAGE SAYS: I am completely accountable and use inventiveness and all the resources and magic of the universe to have what I want.

MY MONEY BAGGAGE: _____   MY MONEY MESSAGE: _____

_____   _____
_____   _____
_____   _____
_____   _____

SITUATION: _____
_____
_____

MONEY BAGGAGE SAYS: _____   MONEY MESSAGE SAYS: _____

_____   _____
_____   _____
_____   _____
_____   _____

SITUATION: _____
_____
_____

MONEY BAGGAGE SAYS: _____   MONEY MESSAGE SAYS: _____

_____   _____
_____   _____
_____   _____
_____   _____

My Money Baggage: _____   My Money Message: _____
_____   _____
_____   _____
_____   _____
_____   _____

Situation: _____
_____
_____

Money Baggage says: _____   Money Message says: _____
_____   _____
_____   _____
_____   _____
_____   _____

Situation: _____
_____
_____

Money Baggage says: _____   Money Message says: _____
_____   _____
_____   _____
_____   _____
_____   _____

ACKNOWLEDGMENTS

I would love to acknowledge my mother and father: June Duncan and Doug Serrill.

Ward Serrill

—

When one starts a journey from the heart, the universe brings the perfect people at the perfect moment into one's life. This has been my experience from day one with this book.

First and foremost is my co-author, Ward Serrill. You took my ramblings and turned them into eloquent jewels. Forever and always I am grateful.

Thank you to Professor Jacob Needleman. In a lifetime I think there are only a few experiences that go on the list of events that are truly life changing. Reading your book and applying your philosophy to my life are on my list. Thank you for your vision and inspiration.

Thank you to Gordon Keating for having the initial conversations with me that sparked the concepts of the book and the first Caring for Your Soul in Matters of Money® workshop ever delivered. You helped me get the ball rolling.

Thank you to all the individuals profiled in the book—you know who you are. Your willingness to take my message to heart, apply it to your lives, and create miracles as a result is truly inspiring. Your willingness to share made the concepts of this book come to life.

Thank you to Dr. Pat Bacilli, Bobbie Baxter, and Bobbi Braden from the Dr. Pat Show, and to Sheila Richardson for introducing us. Thank you all for being the impetus for getting this book done. Thank you for really believing in me and loving the title.

Thank you to Terry Axelrod. Thank you for your willingness to share all that you've learned about publishing books to make the process so much easier. But most of all, thank you for being my best friend and inspiration.

Thank you to Elizabeth Smith on the Benevon™ staff for sharing all your tips and contacts.

Which leads me to the most incredible publishing team anyone could ever wish for. To Kathi and Hobie Dunn at Dunn & Associates Design. Your cover design is exactly what I had envisioned but, because I'm a financial planner, could have never done. You captured the book's essence and created a cover that inspires me each time I look at it.

To Leslie Eliel, editor extraordinaire. You took our baby and brought it to a whole new level. Thank goodness I never have to wonder again where the comma should go. Your ease in working together made the editing a dream. You are the best.

To Paulette Eickman, book designer. I never knew what a difference the design of the interior of a book could contribute to the quality of the finished product. You carried the spirit of the cover and my message to the pages and made it all come together. Terrific.

To the staff at Ramsey & Associates: Shawn Donnelly, John Doherty, Tim Melia, Fabrizio Regoli, and Franky Hartuno. Thank you for your dedication and teamwork. I am honored to work with you each day.

A special thank you to Tara Lemley, the glue that holds Ramsey & Associates together, but much more importantly, my partner in making this dream come true. Your enthusiasm, insight, and laughter are a joy to be around. Want some chocolate?

To the Certified Leaders of the Caring for Your Soul in Matters of Money® workshop: LeAnn Bamford, Janet Belle, Loretta Love Huff, Judy deLena, Pamela Drake, Anita Mark, Oliver Mark, Janie

Morrison, Patty Neilson, Megan Oltman, Mary Ellen Sanajko, Herb Sawin, and Diana Smith. Thank you for letting me coach you and for applying these principles to your lives. It is an honor to know you. Thank you for the contribution you each made to my life and to this book.

Jane Shearer, my dear. Thank you for your unwavering commitment and support. I couldn't do this without you. I love you.

And finally, with deep gratitude to the participants in the Caring for Your Soul in Matters of Money® workshop over the years: Your courage to delve into your money baggage and create your money message moved me then and moves me now. Thank you for the privilege of our interactions and for giving me the opportunity to care for my soul.

Karen Ramsey

REFERENCES

Campbell, Joseph. *The Hero with a Thousand Faces*. Princeton, NJ: Princeton University Press, 1949

Chodron, Pema. *When Things Fall Apart*. Boston: Shambhala Publications, Inc., 1995

Hearn, Michael Patrick. *The Annotated Christmas Carol: A Christmas Carol in Prose by Charles Dickens*. New York: W.W. Norton & Company, Inc., 2004

Hearn, Michael Patrick, ed. *The Wizard of Oz: the Screenplay*, by Noel Langley, Florence Ryerson and Edgar Allen Woolf. New York: Delta (Bantam Doubleday Dell), 1989

Lindbergh, Anne Morrow. *Gift from the Sea*. New York: Pantheon (Random House, Inc), 1955, 1975, renewed 1983 by Anne Morrow Lindbergh

Needleman, Jacob. *Money and the Meaning of Life*. New York: Currency Doubleday (Bantam Doubleday Dell), 1991

Peale, Norman Vincent. *Positive Imagining: The Powerful Way to Change Your Life*. New York: Ballantine Books (Random House), 1982

Shaw, George Bernard. *Man and Superman*. New York: Penguin Books, 1946

Walsch, Neale Donald. *Conversations with God*. Charlottesville, VA: Hampton Roads Publishing Company, Inc., 1995

Winfrey, Oprah. "How I Got There." *Newsweek*, October 24, 2005, 48-49.

ALSO AVAILABLE FROM THE AUTHOR

WORKSHOP: The Caring for Your Soul in Matters of Money® workshop, a life-changing seminar that uses the concepts described in this book, may be available in your area. For information on attending the workshop, visit *www.karenramsey.com* and click on the CARING link. Or, if you would like to sponsor the workshop for your organization's team, please contact:

Ramsey Seminars, LLC
Caring for Your Soul in Matters of Money®
1730 N. Northlake Way, Suite 3301, Seattle, WA 98103
(206) 324-1950
info@caringmoney.com

WORKSHOP LEADERSHIP TRAINING: If you are interested in being trained to lead the Caring for Your Soul in Matters of Money® workshop, or would like us to send information to someone you know, please email *info@caringmoney.com*.

GUEST SPEAKING: Karen Ramsey is an accomplished speaker for organizations, book clubs, and keynote addresses or other events. To learn more or book an engagement, please email *info@karenramsey.com* or visit *www.karenramsey.com* and click on the CARING link.

OTHER BOOKS: *Think Again: New Money Choices, Old Money Myths* shows you how to take control of your finances and realize your dreams. In Part I, Karen challenges the twenty-one most prevalent money myths. In Part II, she outlines her proven, easy-to-follow Personal Spending Plan that will help you get your financial life on track. This book offers exciting new options that can lead to your financial security—without deprivation. For information, please visit *www.karenramsey.com* and click on the THINK AGAIN link.

RAMSEYINVESTING.COM: An online investment management service for portfolios starting at $50,000. *"You don't have to be wealthy to get excellent investment advice."* For information, please visit *www.karenramsey.com* and click on the RAMSEYINVESTING.COM link.

If you would like to share a brief story or any insights that result from working with the concepts in *Caring for Your Soul in Matters of Money®*, please send your story by email to *story@karenramsey.com*.